DEDICATION

I dedicate this book to my loving parents,
Mary and Bob Franz
and to
my wonderful wife,
the love of my life,
Leslie Jeanne Franz.

FOREWARD

Bringing Peace to Violently Troubled Minds

Part 1—Introduction of Problem:

This is a presentation about my book – **_The Stigma of the Mentally Ill: Bob Does Everything Backwards -- Writing Out of an Illness_**.

I am just like a black bear that climbs a suburban tree. All of the humans look up at the bear on the branches, point and say – "We have to tranquilize the bear." The humans say this because of their own needs. Yet, there is nothing wrong with the bear. Why can they not let him go about his own business? Don't they know that in most cases they can?

Some in this society have designated me as mentally ill. Therefore some want me filled with pills. Yet I can trust myself to not be upset and to not be violent. Why can they not let me be myself?

Drugs and medicine are involved from my life, to Charlie Sheen's life, all the way to guys who shoot up victims with bullets and bombs. In certain other cases victims are spared because of the good training and learned behavior of the mentally ill and/or lack of access to weapons. On the other hand, in particular cases where patients are forced and strong-armed to take medicine the result is that strife compounds strife. Kindness and caring are not given and patients are treated harshly. Don't we as humans learn to treat others as we have been treated? What does a patient do when members of the mental health team basically do not like him? What recourse does the individual have?

Let's look at what is really happening. Black bears, like humans, have a hypothalamus in their brain – except that the one in humans is a little larger. In the hypothalamus is a bath of natural brain chemicals that reach a balance and affect behavior. A natural, good work-out can affect these chemicals and positively affect mood and thought. Why then should we ingest complex and unnatural drugs and chemical into our brain systems when many times these foreign drugs have caused aberrant, angry thoughts and erratic violent behaviors?

For example, phenothiazines or major tranquilizers are prescribed to many mental patients. It is very difficult to stop taking many of these antipsychotics once a patient has begun a regimen of this medicine. There is a possibility that brain structure actually changes in patients that have taken these chemicals over time. Withdrawal is difficult and dangerous and can actually reintroduce psychosis.

Tricyclic antidepressants have varying effects. Some antidepressants diminish the desire to use tobacco products and nicotine. But at the same time a patient can feel sudden suicidal ideations which can lead to self-inflicted violence. There is danger with antidepressants especially when one feels the "chemical med rush".

We also know that certain benzodiazepines can cause a "high" and dependence. Withdrawal is strong and freedom is difficult. No one really knows what is going on in an individual when taking 'medicine cocktails' or when one is withdrawing from a substance.

Doctors too, do not always know what is happening. They do not know if patients are consistently taking the medicine prescribed to them. Are they getting "high" on other drugs? In short, it is natural to assume that some people are withdrawing from certain drugs while being "high" on others – a recipe for erratic behavior and more violence.

This is true considering that over 1/5th of the adult population in the United States has been prescribed at least one psychiatric drug at some point in their lives. Black bears do not have these problems.

It is essential to work with realistic, objective psychiatrists when medicine therapy is administered. We need better support and wisdom as to how to get 'On' and 'Off' of chemicals. For those who are rogue, or rebellious, there needs to be more supervision and implicit direction. Doctors are needed in mental health as journeymen who would help and teach apprentice patients.

As far as violence is concerned – I want to make the point that most all species of animals do not kill just for the sake of killing. Certain small cats such as bobcats, lynx and the domesticated 'kitty' stalk and kill more than they would eat – indiscriminately. Humans have this tendency too – just look at the history of the 20th century. Violence can be in most humans and not just the mentally ill. Questions on this issue need to be discussed. We all need more kindness and caring. My wife asks, "What does indiscriminate killing have to do with mental illness?"

I say, "Everything! The human species – all of mankind – is mentally ill."

To stop violence and to bring more peace of mind there may be a small segment of the population who ***should*** ingest balanced medicine. But are we not to consider our ability to learn and 'be trained' to not be rough on each other? The roles of family and education need to step up instead of totally relying on the realms of medicine and religion. Through that active teaching we can learn the dangers of fleeting 'highs' and arduous, treacherous withdrawals.

Psychiatrist's medicines hit society in the mid – 20th century like mud splattering on an electric fan. Many people wanted to try all the new chemicals. Now, in the 21st century, we need to know how to use medicines, while having the prudence to show kindness and caring.

Using principles of moderation we can see that the similarities of our brains outweigh the differences. Our society must now improve at the community level by teaching all individuals values with good science. It is time to take the violence out of our minds.

Part 2—Considered Facts:

Please keep in mind psychologist, Albert Ellis, of the early 20th century who stated that we humans "Disturb ourselves in our own minds when there is nothing else to think about." Many times our minds are disturbed and just need quieting.

Here are some questions and considerations to look at:

- Is the purpose of diagnosis to define prognosis and treatment? If not, then it is just another tool leading to stigma.
- What are the ways of defining stigma and reducing it?
- Do all of us – patients and practitioners – take our parts and understand the personal inventories we take as individuals in the medical system? Are we good to everyone in the system?
- We are taught of "the pills that will cure our ills" and the exaggerated myths of Santa Claus. Why can't we be taught through our family and educational systems of the values of tolerance, patience, kindness and caring when dealing with mental illness?
- Only in recent years have I heard about "mood stabilization." Wouldn't it be healthier to deal with this concept instead of getting all wrapped up in John Hinckley's or Mark David Chapman's 'Mental Constructs?' Mood stabilization – no matter what the aberrant thought – may be an answer to stopping some psychiatric violence.
- In many schools it is now advised to diagnose *autism* at an early age. Please consider that thirty years ago many *bipolar* and *schizophrenic* diagnoses could now be on the *autism* spectrum today.

- In early recovery I did not know how to care for myself with disciplined treatment. How can we teach today's patients to be "Masters of the Ordinary" in their lives?
- We honor our athletes and astronauts – why don't we honor our mental patients who are willing to experiment with trial drugs and new treatment? They are heroes too!
- Personally I want to prove that in my life PTSD affected me early at the age of 21. It was violence perpetrated onto me and not that I was 'developmentally disabled' which caused my mental problems. Now I just want to be a 'normal good guy'.
- We need doctors who can get us 'OFF' of pills as well as those who will get us 'ON' pills.

In conclusion what view has this 'mental illness' given me?

➤ There was a time where I saw a spiritual world with all humans dressed and acting like a troupe of monkeys. It was like watching **Planet of the Apes** with all the apes dressed in robes worshipping in religious orthodoxy.
➤ Furthermore: When I was served another mammal's flesh to eat I felt that we were made to be cannibalistic. Even today these thoughts make me wonder and give me "goose flesh".

Then: upon awakening from this nightmare a change had come over me. I had to take the role of an adult male in society:

1. I had to believe that however small my contribution that it would be of value to our community.
2. I had to know of explicit rules and where they came from: Laws = police, government, and science. Morals and basic tenets = religion, basic spirituality.
3. I had to care for myself – while reaching out to others.

My illness caused me to act younger than I really was – I was truly immature. I had to take the responsibility of disciplining care for myself, something which I had pulled away from as a child and teen-ager. In short, it became necessary to learn grade school and middle school disciplines in young adulthood.

The myths and 'all or nothing' beliefs that the medical and religious realms offered did *not* inspire and then *became* dry. True values that I could hold on to came instead from family and educational areas. You may find my beliefs and values in – *__The Stigma of the Mentally Ill: Bob Does Everything Backwards-- Writing Out of an Illness__*. At this point we must consider what we are to learn and master.

Part 3 – Here is One Solution for Us:

To bring peace to violently troubled minds it is necessary for *every* individual in the community to grow through emotional, mental and spiritual stages.
We need to increase naturally into maturity by progressing through developmental stages. Teachers in school guide us, as we move from [K through 5] grade school, to [6 through 8] middle school. What is learned in these early years is used, in the later maturation of each individual. Even if intellectually we are all not on the same plane; we can be similar in the levels of emotional maturity.

If I do not learn social development at an early age, then I will have to learn it when I am older. For example, biting my nails, pacing, and hedonistic pleasures – I did not stop until my twenties and thirties. As a result I did not stop smoking and drinking until I was almost forty. Substitution of negative ways with good habits and effort, aided me into moving in an improved direction.

It is my assumption that immaturity *begets* violence. A further assumption is that maturity – (as the opposite of immaturity) – can be learned both emotionally and intellectually. This means that strife and violence can be stopped from the outset. We must work to have a good and clean life.

How is this shown?

❖ An image I use is a teddy bear with *a lit fuse on a bomb in his lap.* This not only shows mankind's tendency of innocence versus cruel violence – a dichotomy – but danger as well.
❖ Do we feed the grizzly bear or the teddy bear in each one of us? Just which one is to be dominant? How are we to teach others who are in a quest for development?
❖ It may be true that for this 'race' both 'carrots and sticks' are needed. Yet, for this bear, it is valued that 'honey works better than vinegar'.
❖ I believe the hypothesis that encouragement helps us stand tall and have courage, while inspiration moves to motivate. We must allow for maturity to develop in each individual and supervise those sad souls where it does not grow.

Critical attitudes lengthen the miles, while tolerance and patience bring warm smiles. Peace to you now and always – Thank you very much,

Robert N. Franz

Manuscript by Bob Franz

Thesis:

Currently society, professionals and families, based on observations, decide who is mentally ill and what treatment is necessary for this mental health population. Furthermore, attitudes of self proclaimed, responsible parties create stigma for the mentally ill this preventing wellness.

A healthier approach is to have the client address the cause and definition of mental illness allowing for their own self determined measurable goals to define treatment. This could be accomplished by medicine or psychoanalytic therapy, but must work cognitively and on emotions. Not until an active role is taken will the client reach his full potential

Goals of the client may or may not be mutually agreeable with society, professionals and families. For the client who is able to respond, intervening factors, such as religion and education will play a large part in the improvement of health.

The Stigma of the Mentally Ill:
Bob Does Everything Backwards

People are more interested in you when you are interested in them. When I am willing to open up about my family's dysfunction and my role in it; then this enables you to compare your family with mine. We all can gain when we learn what and what not to do.

Here is my family from my eyes for your study – similarities and not differences.

This work has been written under three titles:

The Stigma of the Mentally Ill: Bob Does Everything Backwards

Eclectic Essays Are Working – one man's view on mental health

Bob Does Everything Backwards -- by a man who writes himself out of an illness.

(In this version reading chapters 7 to 18 comes first and only then does one read chapters 1 through 6.)

Observations:

My writing is friendly to both readers who have never been in mental wards or hospitals and to those who have been in mental domiciles

There is appreciation of difficult situations faced by mental health consumers

There are examples and discussion of how to solve mental health problems without using destructive behaviors.

My writing sees patients and caregivers as people and not problems. It sees healthy relationships and not divisions.

Notes:

All references to the name Jeanne are in actuality Leslie, my wife.

In this writing I never imply that I should choose any specific medicine for anyone else.

I used the assumption that everyone can have at least on outside interest in life. That means that all clients can find at least one other interest to pull them out of themselves.

ABSTRACT OF MANUSCRIPT
Robert N. Franz, May 2009

Chapter	Title
7	Adventures ... Example scenes, gentle patients ... to state hospital, a non-drinking blackout scene
8	Psychosis ... Definitions, mental constructs, mind sets, letters and examples, sensible intake, isolation.
9	More Adventures ... More isolation examples, how some people leave others, doctoring mistakes.
10	Attempts at Success ... Accepting failure, realizing diagnosis, my history, questions, gratitude
11	Not Enough ... Human protests in mental ward, imploding and bombing state hospital
12	Authority ... Walking with Dad, role models, doctors vs clergy, how to lead, treatment and chain of command
13	Rude Awakening ... Letters, thoughts of death, prayer, investigation of Christ, changes spiritually, influences.
14	Angels ... Force for the good, even in my life, Mother, reincarnation, bringing forth.
15	Family ... Apostasy, spiritual morass, aid from another, recognizing importance, who am I? What is my part?
16	Spirituality ... Personal origins, questions, transformation of personality, interview by clergy, random thoughts.
17	Sentiments ... Elders and good attitude, usefulness, clans used helping individuals and bringing cohesive strength, letters to those who have been close.
18	A Message ... High School field trip to Sonoma State Hospital, interview, necessities for patients, 2009 conclusions.
19	The Wedding ...Teddy Bears talk of events and feelings at their wedding.

ABSTRACT OF MANUSCRIPT
Continued

TABLE OF CONTENTS

Chapter	Title	Page

TABLE OF CONTENTS

June 22, 2013

The Stigma of the Mentally Ill:
Bob Does Everything Backwards

Introduction:

This book is about the treatment of my mental health and the search for spirituality as a young adult in late 20th century America. Relationships with doctors and clergy as well as family and society influences are examined. I describe what does and does not work for me. Listed here are introductory facts which aid in the understanding of the experiences represented in Bob Does Everything Backwards.

My Mother and other members of my original family have given me an appreciation for the arts. Expression has come to us through the emotions shown in the culture of art, music and theater. I want to pay this culture forward.

Vincent Van Gogh was one of the artists my Mother focused on as she appreciated his tortuous work. When others of his genre painted on canvas to their perfection; his expression showed schizophrenia. While others accepted or rejected his work; he was lost at the end of his life.

In my scientific studies I have come across a book by Victor Frankel, Man's Search for Meaning which describes torture methods used by the Nazi's. Frankel's readership was forgiving of his theories because of what he endured in wartime Germany. Frankel's "empirically scientific" theories were just as faulty as Van Gogh's paintings, yet each man could be respected because of the appreciation of each man's struggle.

Just as certain artists and scientists are respected for their past so I also ask for respect for my many years in and out of mental hospitals in modern day America. My three years as a patient in mental domiciles were peppered by stints out the hospitals as I "tried to make it" without much human help or support.

As my thoughts would have it, I have compiled Bob Does Everything Backwards first by writing everything I felt needed changing in our system. As I wrote and honed down chapters one through six I realized that they were strong enough to use as an ending and subsequently I used them in anger _as_ an ending. Hence, Bob _really_ does do everything backwards. This ending explains what has to be accomplished in America to bring an acceptable answer to the problem of mental illness

I continued to write stories from my past true in my memory. When putting them on paper I kept the ones which were important to my medical history or my spiritually inspired well being. I showed this writing to a couple of friends who commented on my work.

The first friend told me that I made my point in chapters 7 though 18, but that people would have a difficult time reading the manuscript because it seemed as a schizophrenic would write – disjointed. Respecting my friend's opinion, I have worked to change this

17

shortcoming. It was right to say that my illness affected my writing and that I could actually be diagnosed by my written word. But, a more accurate way to see this is that my writings reflect my illness and therefore the discerning eye could see the defects or faults which make me prone to mental illness.

As a result I chose personal scenes which typified my experience as a mental patient. They did not always jive together but as a unit they described what was happening to me. Later I went back and chose consistent names to some characters to add continuity and character development. The scenes, thoughts, and struggles I have described in the work show my journey to medical and spiritual answers. These are chronicled in the first part of my book, which includes chapters 7 through 18 – again writing from back to front.

At the same time I wrote an account for the psychiatric journal, Psychiatric Services, (8/1999) and was edited by Jeffrey L. Geller, M.D., M.PH. Not only did Dr. Geller have suggestions as an editor but by "tweaking" a few of my personal scenes he made them more readable. I am so grateful – I am forever grateful. Now I have the respect of being noticed and the means to clarity my life. Understanding begins and answers are forthcoming at a personal level.

Although this book does not concern itself per se with gun background checks, it should be know that one out of a dozen or so of my psychiatrists had diagnosed me as "paranoid schizophrenic," a most troubling and violent branding view of a man. Not only was this psychiatrist's diagnosis wrong, but in truth my psychiatric state has morphed for the better throughout the years.

Even now I feel that when alone I am being watched by specific mysterious people. This belief has gone on for years but as I become older I feel the presence of more understanding "watchers."

The "watched Bob" means that I am always checking to see my part in every situation aware to me. I act appropriately practically 100% of the time because I always feel a presence. If you cannot beat it then just go with it. Acceptance is the key. I never have the feeling that I can "get away with something" because I know people will know all about me. I do not smoke or drink and these disciplines must be done perfectly.

Look at our society: Paparazzi with celebrities, secret service with politicians, cameras on the corners and in the stores, millions watching a putt. Even the pope has been a bouncer in a nightclub. We are all being watched so much of the time. If you assume that you are always being watched you are one step ahead of the game. Be prepared.

The paranoia secret is not the only secret I live by. My brain has to know where to go. I am like a commercial airliner on auto-pilot or a missile to a target. As I travel; there are discreet adjustments continually made. I want to be a better person yet the end target comes only after continued adjustments are made. My goal is to be accurately understood as a writer.

When I was young I would confront others and rebel by standing out for attention. I would rebel at what I thought were my "watchers." Now I take my part and fit in better. I try to understand others more readily. I do my job and my part while trying to release myself from "the bondage of self". Paranoia is not the issue – understanding others become more dominant. A functional part of society is something I can become.

My wife Leslie Jeanne likes to read fictional (based on fact) detective stories that are written in omniscient or all-knowing style. I tend to write in omniscient style because I have a know-it-all streak in me and because I am confident. To do this I write in both first and third person tenses.

Another friend has told me that in these writings she was distracted by my use of both first and third person tenses. Again I respect my friend's opinion but I feel that in this case it is necessary. I write in the first person to show my feelings, thoughts, and actions. I write in the third person to have some distance to critique my behavior and environment. Although I can and do criticize others I try to judge and criticize mainly myself. This is done to watch and check my behavior as I fit in society.

When I use the first person I am expressive and want to stand out. When I use the third person I want to see my part and want to fit in. My behavior is cyclical.

There may be psychiatric reasons for the use of different tenses. Remember, I do have a diagnosis. You may be able to diagnose me from my writing without knowing me in person. Maybe there is more than one affective shortcoming.

By writing in the omniscient style I can show the many perspectives of a problem. There are varied views. Although I try to move in a healthy direction, I do not always know where my brain is directed. You have to know that I do not think and speak in paragraphs. Fortunately though, there are times when humor will surface. At least when I talk this way to our cat Misty – she seems to understand.

By all perspectives I have shown in this book that I was correct in my estimation of medical and spiritual theories given to me in my youth. I have not desired to have the realization of the self-pity that I was getting screwed by these entities. I do not want to admit to getting screwed and neither do I want anyone else to get screwed as well. Hopefully we can prevent harm being done to people. It is hard to accept that these disciplines are not perfect and that one cannot get well all of the time.

I got screwed by a couple of medical professionals. Research in the offing does not always give what is promised. My church was not as bad. Spiritually I had to lose old "Santa" stories but these were nothing to lose compared to what other people had to face from their churches. All in all both in the medical and spiritual – expectations for people were made way too high for comfort.

I wish to be open and will not hide any mental illness in me. For me to get well through this writing I have to use the muscle of the mind and face all sickness. I have to write with the intent to change myself and how I see the world.

It was necessary for me to make chapters 7 through 18 more natural and have more flow. I developed characters by have them re-appear in the text. I included little vignettes or scenes which told of meaning, and finally I tapped into American culture by referencing John Wayne films and The Wizard of Oz as is written by L. Frank Baum.

Dorothy, the Good Witch Glinda, and the Wicked Witch Bastinda's names were all used. The first names of actors in The Wizard of Oz were utilized in my text: Judy for Dorothy, Bert for the Cowardly Lion, Jack for the Woodsman, and Ray for the Scarecrow. By doing this I bring a personal journey in which we all can identify.

I cannot forget the few real people to me who are in my account of <u>Bob Does Everything Backwards</u>. Without my wife Leslie Jeanne Franz I would not even be living. You should notice that sometimes she is called Leslie and sometimes Leslie Jeanne. She is very real and dearly loved by me.

Mary and Bob Franz Jr. are my loving and loyal parents as Annette is my loving, efficient, competent and concerned sister. All three are so very important to me.

Eric is my son (stepson) and Ernie is my father-in-law. We have worked together throughout the years for the positive as we all improve.

Karen Kovacic M.D., V. Gurijala M.D., Kenneth Weller M.D., and Susan Poritsky M.D. have been positive doctors to me. There are other unmentioned good doctors and therapists.

There are three clergy from the Diocese of Wilmington needing mentioned. One is the Reverend John Klevence who interviewed me, along with pastors Reverend James Kirk and Reverend Michael Carrier of the Church of the Holy Child. Happily included are many clergy in Delaware who bring life to the Word.

Many people who are good for the body and soul go unmentioned who have influenced the writing of this book. I hope that we all can work together in positive ways to accept and aid the many mentally ill in our midst. Even the "Worried Well" could use a little help. Go to it.

This introduction of <u>Bob Does Everything Backwards</u> is now complete. I will be giving copies of it to people who I think may want to read my work. If you do not wish to read anymore of this then do not say anything. But, on the other hand, if you do, then let me know and I will supply you with a most ameliorating, healthy way of looking at life. Read the book... Please!

Most sincerely,

Robert N. Franz III

Bob – The author of this text was kidded by his friends in college by having them say to him that he "backed into everything he did." Not only did he back into parking lot scrapes; he backed into writing, (Bob never intended to write a book) as well as his best swim stroke is the elementary backstroke, which looks like an octopus when it tries to escape from danger by pushing its head back and spraying ink like clouds as an oceanic smoke screen.

Here and now when you read this work, I have arranged it so you read the second half first and the first half second. It is right to read the writing in this way. It is just the 'write' thing to do.

Please look closely at the table of contents to know what Bob means by "writing himself out of an illness backwards". He saw where he had ended up and traced it backwards. By writing this way he could see where he had been and how his personality changed over time, but as the book is shown to you the reader, it makes more sense to see the transformation in this way. So, in presenting the story to the reader, Bob especially wanted to make the point that he had to travel backwards.

Chapters 7 to 11 which begin the work state clearly where Bob was: lost in a world of mental illness. Then chapters 12 through 19 define what actually happened to Bob's personality. Finally chapters 1 through 6 reveal a change which proves that many people may be healed or at the least are able to change dramatically with similar work.

Perhaps others can use this way of writing to trace a change. Certainly in writing the authors go from point to point. It is also important to know what direction the authors are traveling. Perhaps it could be noted that our travels in writing are not always linear. A story – or even a dream – can have a trajectory of a parabolic cannonball while another could float to earth as on a path that a feather would fall. Each author, in fact each story, would have its own movement. We should not conform to just one way. Perspective comes from knowing where to turn and look.

Finally please know that when in doubt, or when an important event or milestone comes in the course of a lifetime, it is wise to pause, take a couple of steps backwards and avail yourself of perspective which moves you carefully and wholly forward. This includes the safety factor known as prudence.

Please enjoy this book if you can.

TEDDY BEARS OR BOMBS ~
WHICH DO YOU WANT?

In Defense of the Teddy Bear Connection

There have been some complaints about the teddy bears in this book. Some say that they say too much of what will happen, or are too preachy, or more to the point they are 'disingenuous'.

Frankly, the teddy bears are here because they are meant to wake you up. I want to pique the reader's interest.

Don't you know that in this society everyone wants to be on top? Everyone wants to "deign" to explain. Haven't you ever seen people talk down to those in wheelchairs? Mt. Everest just has too many climbers. It is too crowded for safety and comfort. I feel that it is about time that people go easier on each other. If there were more smiles all of our miles would be more comfortable to handle.

The teddy bears are a warning for us all. Why does everyone know better than everyone else? Teddy bears are the opposite of bombs. One attracts caring – the other explodes violently. You have a choice – do you want it soft or hard?

My use of teddy bears shows my frustration of having people talk down to me throughout this life. It's got a lot to do with Gandhi and Martin Luther King Jr. Do you want bombs or soft teddy bears? Which one do you want? How else can we bring peace?

Starting

Starts,

Starts, and Starts,

Starts and Starts and more Starts,

As a Long Journey with Stoplights,

As a Revved Up Drag Racer;

"You can always start again."

As a Sprint,

As a Heartbeat Starting Over and Over,

As Daybreak

Starts.

Yes Start,

As it should be

Now,

As a Forgiven Soul

Robert Franz   1994

SEVEN

ADVENTURES

"Teribear, if I could give anything from this ole' schizoaffective bear to the obsessive-compulsive you, it would be that order will come out of confusion. Just read these next five chapters and keep in mind the internal struggles versus the external ones. All of the difficulties play mental, physical, emotional, and spiritual roles. Once I can handle the confusion life becomes much simpler." Ted E. Bear said.

"As an OCD patient I should be able to see what you just said." Continued Teribear, "For we are organizing all the time."

"Be advised – some of these times I have the lowest self-esteem that I ever had in my life. I am lonely and afraid."

"Oh, Mr. Ted E. Bear, I hate to see you so down," cried Teribear.

Whether it's for the better or not, my personality has changed a great degree over the years. Specifically I am more serious, and do not laugh near as much at the expense of others. Also, I feel an urge to contribute and desire results that express how I feel.

In the fall of 1978 I learned that I could be weak yet still be effective in relating to people. It was also shown that one could be knee-shaking afraid, yet brave at the same time. Before that time when I was afraid I just went along with the crowd. To do that today would be a mistake.

Leslie Jeanne had light azure blue eyes and brunette hair. At one time she was a receptionist. Her stature was tiny, demure, and others called her petite. I really could not say that we hit it off right away because communicating with her was very difficult in the private mental institution. Besides, however quick she was inside, she was very slow on the outside. Every now and then Leslie Jeanne would just stop whatever she was doing and just sit motionless. Although she did not like this expression it seemed as though she was "striking a pose." I do not know what was wrong with her and right now I am not going to conjecture, but something made me want to protect her and care for her at the same time.

I was weak from being in the state hospital. Weak, I say, because in the state hospital I was terrified of others and I did not feel the staff was looking after the best interests of the patients. I would stay up at night fearful of the next day. Even at mealtime food was taken off my plate by others. For a time, I became a real 'wimp,' and was ashamed. My insurance allowed me to go to the private hospital so I jumped at the chance. During my stay there I met Leslie Jeanne. Her insurance only had one more month before stopping benefits. Leslie Jeanne would have to be admitted to a state hospital for an undetermined period of time if she did not get any better. I became fearful for Leslie Jeanne and did not want to scare her by talking about the state hospital. Instead, I watched her – especially with her psychiatrist.

Dr. Tinman spent the same amount of time with Leslie Jeanne as with other patients. He appeared to be a very caring and patient man. Most likely he knew there wasn't much time to get Leslie Jeanne to speed up her actions before transferring hospitals, but he did not rule it out either. Soon he brought a typewriter to our ward just for Leslie Jeanne's use and one could see him talking to her and then waiting, waiting, for a response. It was always difficult to wait for a response from the gentle Leslie Jeanne.

One day, in a crowded day room, a new female patient looked over the typing of Leslie Jeanne and said, "Why she's only typed three and half sentences in a half hour! I've been watching her. I'm going to use this typewriter if that's all she's going to do." With that the new patient began to use the typewriter.

Leslie Jeanne began crying with sincere tears, "You don't understand, you don't understand. I need the typewriter. I need to *type*." With that, she slowly went back to her room waiting for the day that was coming so soon. "Why isn't anyone listening to me?" This "outcry" was the most I ever heard from her.

The next morning the typewriter was taken from the ward and a floor meeting was called by Dr. Tinman. All the patients on the ward were to hear what was happening about Leslie Jeanne leaving the hospital. Afterwards, I told Dr. Tinman my concerns about Leslie Jeanne going to the state hospital.

"She's too gentle to go there," I said.

He replied, "She can't go anywhere else."

"I don't know what will happen to her. She'll get swamped."

"Now you are making me wonder, because that's what happened to you. They've assured us that she will be OK. What happened to you there is another matter."

"I know I wasn't acting confident at all in the state hospital."

"Exactly, you were acting in fear, and I have seen you do that. Even Leslie Jeanne knows your fear. I suggest you work with you doctor to rid yourself of that fear."

"Thank you, but that is just another assignment."

"Good Luck."

For me, there was plenty to think about. There still is.

In four days Leslie Jeanne packed her bags and with her family went to the state hospital. I still cannot believe how brave she was in walking out those doors. She came up to me and said, "Thank you for everything Bob, Thank you." And I did not know even what I had done for her. All I could do is blink back tears and nod my head. I felt the abyss of mental illness was getting lost in the abyss of social warehousing. Please, Lord, let her get out someday.

It's been four years since I have given serious thought to Leslie Jeanne. In that time I have been trying to work on my fears instead of superficially covering them up. I have recognized that hope gives strength and not the other way around. Also, I see that both hope and strength can come after a trial or period of weakness.

But the quality I see most of all is hope, and look forward to life. It doesn't depend on the packaging of the individual; it depends on what is inside. Leslie Jeanne was willing to try her best.

There have been times in my life when I have been willing to try my best but because of bad decision-making all I have ever done is succeed in exhausting myself. I signed out of a hospital and alcohol rehabilitation center and walked the streets of Wilmington. Something or someone protected me in those days.

Whether I was in the hospital – which had a rehab attached to it – or walking the streets one thing was certain; I was totally consumed with myself. I became so utterly sick and tired of always thinking of myself that in the end I sipped insecticide in an attempt to kill myself. I could not, however, force myself to drink the stuff. I only wanted to die.

Let me begin by saying how I got to the Sunday Breakfast Mission of Wilmington, Delaware in a chilly November of 1981. That fall I had seen Leslie Jeanne again but on this occasion things were different. I had now known her in the biblical sense for almost three months.

It seemed cold for November but the weather was changing to be slightly warmer. I was in a mental hospital – rehab in Norristown Pennsylvania and my doctor had reduced my medicine. This gave me enough room to function but too little to make any sense. I knew I knew had to follow the rules, but as a practical joker I replaced toothpaste tubes with Preparation H tubes for other patients. Once my medicine level came down I felt well enough to leave no matter what anyone would say. So I signed a 24 hour notice form letting me legally leave in 24 hours. The doctor was insistent and told me that if I leave that he would never take me back.

Twenty-four hours came and went and by the next evening I left in a suit and tie with my suitcase. I hitched rides to Wilmington giving one man 40 dollars to drop me off at a local Howard Johnson's restaurant. Finally I called a number of friends and one of them agreed to drive me to a young woman's apartment who I knew from nursing school (Leslie Jeanne). At this point I was getting on everyone's nerves because I was so demanding and manipulative. Leslie Jeanne would take me in I thought, or at least she would be glad to see me.

Before leaving the hospital, I spoke on the phone to my parents and they said under no uncertain terms was I to come to their home if I were to sign out of the hospital. I did not want to anyway. The doctor did not want anything to do with me either if I were to leave. The people I called on the phone did not really care to help me on my terms either. Finally the fellow who took me to Newark, Delaware told me that this was the last time he was going to do anything for me. Blithely I went on.

Secretly, I knew that Leslie Jeanne would be different. On one date four months earlier with her we talked about moving to Arizona and starting over. Couldn't I rekindle anything with her, or was it all day dream? What would she say if I showed up at her door with a suitcase? It was going to happen. Believe me, if a spaceship had shown up I would boarded and paid for the ticket. I was then dropped off at Leslie Jeanne's apartment. Here I am, I thought. "Be positive, just be positive." I hid my suitcase outside her door and rang the bell. She answered.

"Avon calling" I said.

"Yea right." she said, "Now you're selling cosmetics."

"You should see my line of products."

"I always knew you had one" she replied with a smile.

"I never thought I'd have to use it -- especially now, for you."

"Well you just did and I want to know why, so come in and tell me."

Here was my chance to tell her of all the horrendous things that have happened to me. Here was my chance to make her feel sorry for me. I better go slowly, not act sick and maybe we could go to Arizona sometime soon. Also, I believed I was proving to myself, in front of Leslie Jeanne that I could live without the psychotic medicine which I had taken for so long. Just give me another chance off this medicine. I knew that I could think my way through the aberrant thoughts that would result.

We had just sat down to her dinner, which was already in progress, with her young child Eric. He was the precious charge that Leslie practiced her affections on. Eric's real father would pass when Eric was in his late teens. His Dad respected others and even though he did not marry Leslie – he showed caring and affection towards Eric. Living separately from his son he loved Eric from a distance for the first 18 years of Eric's life. In kind, Eric judged other men by the stature of his father. It is important to know that many boys truly think highly of their dads and wish to emulate them.

Soon a knock came from the door. It was a man who lived across the drive in the apartments – a boyfriend to be sure Leslie Jeanne rose abruptly and put her finger across her lips signaling me to be quite.

"Whose suitcase is this?" the man asked.

Leslie Jeanne replied, "It must be ours."

"It must be yours," he said sarcastically, "What do you do, just pick up strange men and take them in? Come here and talk to me."

With that Leslie Jeanne stepped outside and talked to this man for a few minutes. Then she came inside with my suitcase. At first I felt overjoyed because it looked like I had made the first step in a journey; later, as we talked I realized that she was not paying full attention to my story. She was preoccupied and teary-eyed, and I knew something was going to happen. Mentally, I braced myself for the worst. I looked out the window and saw the flashing lights of a lone police car. Soon, there was a rap at the door.

Actually it was only one county policeman who was at first very official and polite. He talked to the man across the way and then he talked to Leslie Jeanne. At one point she said to me that I was doing her a favor by showing up at her apartment at this moment in time. I did not understand the statement. But, it had to do with the man across the way and his jealousy. I was in a suit and the other man wore grungy old jeans and a T-shirt so it became obvious why the policeman kept calling me "Sir". Leslie Jeanne also, seemed to hold me in high esteem because I did everything she said. I was 'following instructions'. I just stayed in the apartment when the man accused me of being on drugs. I stayed near the suitcase and only opened it when the police told me to do so. I would agree with all of Leslie Jeanne's accounts of how we knew each other from nursing school. Finally, the policeman told me to come with him and he would find me a place to stay for the night. Leslie Jeanne gave me a big hug as other police questioned the man who lived across the apartment drive. My hope was in the future – if not with Leslie Jeanne then with someone else. I felt needed.

At that point in time I knew I would have to leave with the county cop and became afraid that he would take me to the state hospital. He said that he had other plans for me. It was 10:30 pm and something had to happen quickly. Leslie Jeanne and the other man were with another county cop having an argument in front of her place. I had no time to talk (or even think) when the cop whisked me off in his cruiser thankfully without handcuffs.

The county cop said, "Do you want to go to a motel or the Mission?"

"I only have about 40 dollars. Better not go to a motel." After a pause I continued, "What is the Mission?"

"It's a place where transients can sleep. Sort of like a humble bed and breakfast."

"But, where is it?"

"It's in downtown Wilmington, I'll show you. You'll have to leave in the morning after they wake you and of course after a couple of donuts."

"Speaking of food I completely forgot to eat dinner tonight."

"Hmm," replied the cop, "Let's stop and get something. Here's a good spot." He drove into the parking lot of a donut shop, left the car, and returned with a dozen donuts. "Call it dinner if you want. I'll call ahead on my radio and make sure there is a bed for you at the Mission."

As I wolfed down the donuts the cop told me how I did a favor for Leslie Jeanne, but that he was not willing to talk about it. He also asked me if I wanted to become a lawyer that he would do what he could to help me. I was just happy to be talking to someone other than doctors, nurses, and patients even if he did seem too friendly. As we drove around the train station toward the Mission he finally told me to go to Traveler's Aid Station the very next day if I need help and that they would get me on a bus to Dover or some other location. I still was bound and determined to make it on my own without the help of family.

The Mission is a one story building that houses 200 men with bars on all its windows and doors. In large yellow neon letters one can see "The Sunday Breakfast Mission" spelled out. To the side is a thrift shop. To the other side are vacant houses.

Each day 180 of these men leave at seven in the morning and are suppose to return, if they want a bed, at four in the afternoon. Each day they must listen to an hour sermon, receive dinner and go to a bunk for the night. This night, I missed the sermon and dinner, and because they were doing a favor for the police, I was accepted to sleep on a bunk. The other twenty men are called residents, have their own rooms, and received stipend for completed tasks around the Mission. That night I aspired to be a resident.

Something must be said of my mental state. Since I was not taking medicine I began to go into my own world. I felt time machines were affecting my life. I felt aliens would come and get me in the night and take me to other coordinates. I felt there would be a major relief in the morning. I slept in my suit and when I took off my shoes the guy in the bunk beneath me complained of the stench from my socks. So I put my good shoes back on and slept that way.

At five in the morning a resident tried to rouse me three times. I finally arose at six with most of the men on their way out of the building. Hastily showering in freezing cold water I dressed with everyone yelling at me to hurry up. It was a relief to walk out of the building in the cold November air even with a large hard side Samsonite suitcase. With fantasy thoughts of spaceships in my mind I just walked.

Just then, four young men converged on me. One pulled a knife and demanded whatever I had. They took my wallet and the last amount of change I had, but left me with my suitcase. Rifling through my pockets the leader said, "If you tell anyone we'll kill you." Then they left quickly behind a building leaving me with my suitcase. I ran down the street with it until I could go no further. Wanting a cigarette I cried out of loneliness. I told the next person I saw that there was a spaceship coming. Noticing a strange look in him at the sound of my words I decided it best to keep my mouth shut.

What was it that I had to remember? There was something I had to do I thought as pains of hunger hit my stomach. The cop last night said something about Traveler's Aid. Was I a traveler? Did I need help? As far as I could see I needed to talk to someone who could be civil to me in a conversation. I decided to go to Traveler's Aid, asking bystanders and merchants who would not treat me as a street person with difficulty. Finally two people told me where Travelers Aid was located and I headed in that direction. In this time, I must have had ten people call me names or tell me that the suitcase I was toting was not mine or stolen. I prayed for that spaceship to come for me now.

The streets are a harsh place as I was finding out in my one day on them. No one can be trusted unless you find the right place. For me, Traveler's Aid was it. That was my hope.

Overhearing derogatory comments from passersby's became the norm as I got closer to the building. Even using a circular route from the Mission to Traveler's Aid the journey was still less than two miles. I had blisters on my feet and hands from walking and carrying the suitcase. Finally I reached my destination. A worker handed me a ticket. I said,

"What is this for? I don't want to see a movie."

"What do you think it's for?" the worker replied.

"I have no idea."

"What is more basic than a movie?"

"For me? Checking these clothes and a suitcase."

"What is more basic than that?" she said

"I don't know… I honestly don't know."

"Try lunch. Try food."

"Oh yeah, you are so right. I need to eat."

"Take this ticket and get a hot lunch three blocks over. You can't miss it."

I had to wait forty-five minutes but I didn't care. The casseroles were excellent. It was the best hot lunch I think I ever had. Full and refreshed I made my way back to the worker at Traveler's Aid. But this did not stop the rapid-cycling of my mental illness. She listened to my story – not the story of my day – but the story of my mental health. I did not say the right words. All I needed to do is make a phone call to my doctor as I thought I could go back to the Norristown hospital. I knew of nothing else to do. I waited and begged and pleaded with that worker to use her phone to see if my doctor would take me back. Finally she let me call long distance to Pennsylvania. I sat in the waiting room all afternoon for a return call that never came.

My mind had begun to play tricks on me. I did not see, but believed, that a giant preying mantis was stalking me. I began shaking in fright right there in the waiting room. Since no one else was there I checked all corners, closets, and behind the furniture for hiding places. Each time a cloud covered the sun I asked that the good Lord send a spaceship so

I could leave. Talking to this worker I had to keep it together so she would not call the attendants to take me to the state hospital.

Four o'clock in the afternoon came and went. I could not go back to the mission for sleep. By all accounts I was in the hell of mental illness thinking solely of giant preying mantis and spaceships. Things were getting worse and I was serious and tense. Then the worker gave me a phone number I recognized – Dad's work number.

"To call it is the only way," she said.

"But what of my honor," I replied.

"What do you mean?" she asked.

"I want to do it without my parents."

"When a person is in need of a hot meal are they going to deny themselves of that?"

"OK I'll try it, but I don't expect much."

"You won't know until you try."

I called my Dad. His voice sounded caring. I broke down and wept even on the phone. The worker had to leave the room. Within forty-five minutes Dad and I were in a car to my parent's house.

Throughout the years Dad has heard my stories of psychosis. I have told him many times of what I had been "thinking about." So once he learned that I had no medicine – that I believed a giant invisible 'Praying Mantis' was following us, and that a spaceship would save us, he became very sad. With so many hard yet soothing words he talked me out of these beliefs, at least for the time being. Then he told me that I'd have to go back to the hospital for further treatment.

I could see hope waning in his eyes as he had to admit that his only son was mentally ill. I guess at that time upon seeing me without medicine he knew in his heart that I couldn't take care of myself unless I learned how to discipline treatment for myself. Not only could he see my aberrant thoughts but he could see the rapid cycling of my moods. At one minute I could be high and happy and at the next I would be sad and serious. I on the other hand, just explained it by not really being a street person.

The short term hopes were coming through. I had food, a place to sleep and family. But the long term hope of not being mentally ill would not go away. Deep in my heart I knew this, for without medicine my imagination went astray and hurt me. The giant preying mantis turned into an invisible preying mantis with every creak in the wood floors of my parent's house. Two days later I was to go back to the Norristown PA hospital.

My mental state had me in a temporary condition of depression. I began sipping insecticide which I found in the garage because I did not have the guts to "do myself in." I would not pray, for I did not feel that it would work. Reading, television, was out of the question so I just paced. I worried about my future in that wait for a bed at the hospital. Finally my time came and I was to go the next day. Mom would drive.

"I'm doing this as much for myself as I am for you," she told me firmly.

"Doing what?" I said.

"All I'm going to tell you is that we are making a stop on the way to the hospital," she replied. With that we sped off next morning.

After miles of driving we stopped in Maryland at a retreat house where I received the Anointing of the Sick from a clergyman. This surprised me by making me calmer, more accepting, and perhaps some would say, stronger. Even if I did not know if there was a God or not, it sure made me wonder. At least I had hope. The next stop was the hospital.

These four days affected me more than I knew. It clearly showed what effect it had on me when I am off medicine. They show me the harshness of the world and my own vulnerability. It taught me that if I had an undaunted spirit, then I can have hope. Finally, I am taught to ask forthrightly and honestly when I need help. I do not have to live my life alone. Although hope starts as a spark in each individual, it needs nurturing by many. Hope soothes a troubled soul. Thank you, Mom.

Sometimes a Mother is the only one who knows what to do.

Where was my love?

"Teribear? Oh Teribear," said Ted E Bear, "are Bob and Leslie Jeanne ever going to get together?"

"Just wait," Teribear replied, "It takes time and separation to let hearts meld. They will find answers, but first Bob has to reckon with his youthful years and what they will mean for the future."

"I suppose you mean that he has to learn about his aberrant thoughts – that tendency for psychosis?"

"Yes," she states, "Not only from the cranial juices – but from the withdrawal of the drugs they give him."

"Finally, that *is* a problem."

"Yes – they won't get together for awhile."

EIGHT

PSYCHOSIS

"What I do not understand is what I do not understand and I will never understand it." I speak now of psychosis and describe with anecdotes and examples just what motivates my behavior when ill.

What is psychosis? What causes psychosis? These are the questions I wish to answer. Apparently psychosis is caused by a chemical imbalance in the brain and not by some psychological disturbance. I say this because head injury, fever, jolts of electricity, drugs, sleep, and mental illness can all cause the disturbance. To me, all pathological psychosis does not leave quickly and is more than passing. It is not fair to say that an eccentric uncle or a comedian is always psychotic. I'm not too sure about rapists and axe murderers, although they too have a disorder of the mind, which is the definition of psychosis.

In this chapter are letters and essays authentic to the time of my psychosis years ago. Each piece of "evidence" demonstrates what I was thinking at each point in time. This writing also shows what happens when I get off my medicine and can be a good introduction for those who are not familiar with psychosis – or the sickness of the mind. It should be further noticed that I do not hear voices nor have I ever heard voices. Instead I have built up 'constructs' or belief systems in my mind that are based on sophistic reasoning. An example of this is to really believe that an acquaintance of mine was actually a popular singer in disguise. Nothing but time could sway me from this belief. When I got back on the proper medicine this belief slowly left me.

As shown by the following conversation, the first time this happened was terrifying.

"What were you thinking about?" said the prospective girlfriend when I was 22 years old.

"When I was 20 years of age and off this medicine I had so much fear that I felt like ever male in the world wanted to stock something up my lower orifice. Really, Bastinda, I felt like wherever I went someone was going to rape me."

"That's ridiculous, Bob, you knew it wasn't true."

"Not so, Bastinda, I had a mindset about sex and a mental construct that homosexuals ruled the world. I could not change how I felt. Don't you see? It was my own conflict played on the world. My young adult, homophobic feelings [– which I would have had whether I was psychotic or not --] were being projected onto others. If I would have let them pass I would have grown out of these feelings. That's true of almost all psychotic thought constructs within me."

"This is too much for me to take," replied Bastinda.

34

"What do you mean? I am the one taking it," I said. "Many people have written about fantasy or psychosis (not to be used interchangeable) in that they can be used as an escape."

Continuing I said, "This is real torture isolating an individual completely. It is not pretty at all and it has been the ruin of many. My Christian Science friends have looked at it as a soul weakness – both mental and spiritual. Yes, it is vulnerability to the maximum but I do not feel it is caused by some spiritual sin. As evidenced by the medicine it seems to be a nervous, biochemical disorder, most likely dealing with neurotransmitters in the nerves and brain. The practicing Christian Scientists would call it 'not real'."

One of the better colloquial definitions of psychosis is that neurotics build castles in the air where psychotics live in the castles. The psychotic will play with the thought in his mind much more so than others and will keep rehashing or obsessing until he is fooled into believing all aspects. I have defined *mental constructs* as the architecture of the psychosis. These are the actual mechanisms of time machines, clones, UFO's aliens and more. On the other hand, *mind sets* describe the resolve to action or inaction on the part of the psychotic. The mind set determines what behaviors the psychotic will use to cope given the circumstances to undo stress.

It is true that psychotics feel a tremendous amount of fear and anger. In my case, I usually desire a confidante to describe my feelings and thoughts. But this can only work with a trusted person nearby or else the psychotic behavior continues. My most glaring example of this occurred when I was twenty-one in Los Angeles. For four days I was psychotic and not until I saw my Dad who flew out from the east coast did I start reality based behavior. Now I will tell of the constructs of my psychosis of 1992-93.

Personally, what needed to be accomplished was to purge myself of all borderline, psychotic thoughts. These thoughts would come through my mind in a circular fashion each a little different than it came in before. For example – I actually felt that George H. Bush was the clone of King George – or Prince Charles relative. George therefore would sell off the United States back to England unless of course he died prematurely. I knew that was fallacious – I knew I was sick – but it turned around the next time I had a thought about how Barbara Bush was an All-American heroine for how she controlled George. Therefore, there was no need for George to die prematurely. If there was a reason for him to die the better part of me would think up reasons why he shouldn't die. I always had a flip side to psychosis – two stories each with their own scenario. Just wait long enough for an equally fallacious story to cross the mind.

Next is a "Dear God" letter that was written in 1992.

Dear God:

Why have you made me the way I am? Why have I been tortured by going into hospitals so often? I cannot count the times I've thrown it all away in career and school changes. I cannot count the times I've energetically pulled up hard and started something new. Season's changes with personal pressures seem to be a good instigator of bad luck. My hate for IT causes me to not get along with others. God, I try not to be greedy for anything or anyone but I really look for security. My ways and personal habits can put me in the hospital. So now let me describe to you practically everything that happens when I am put into the hospital.

First, medicine changes you one way or the other. The doctors change my medicine – or in the case of Clozaril it makes me too sleepy so I don't take it. They take away what works and I have to adjust all over again to something new.

Second, my mood swings are exacerbated and there are anger riffs with those who are close. I become isolated.

Third, I get a belief system in my head as if I've met Gloria Estefan or that I am swimming in an onshore dolphin pod.

Fourth, work becomes so boring and tedious that I become listless, or pick an argument, or do something dramatically stupid.

Fifth, when people do catch on and try to reach out I'm at the point where all I can do is reject them – especially the meddling doctors.

Sixth, I become grandiose and see people as very good or very bad.

Seventh, my tenseness is very high, and love and jealousy become much stronger.

Eighth, trust leaves and loneliness sets in. I am alone.

HELP ME!!

Please,

Bob

A variety of disorders include, as a symptom, psychosis. Another definition of this word is that one is not in touch with reality. When I am too 'high' in a bipolar phase I can become psychotic.

This chapter thoroughly describes essays and letters of what it was like for me in 1993. Many thoughts go through my mind at a fast pace, yet all of them are based with a shaky foot in reality. From thoughts of meeting a 'look-alike' Gloria Estefan, to George H. Bush, all of these topics in my mind were sad accounts of a cruel disease. I write them so others will know just what this does to a person.

It has been quite awhile since 1993 and Leslie Jeanne and I have time to reflect. Under great stress we separated for 3 months that year. Even when we reconciled we had a lot of healing to do. We did this together and saw not only medicine work, but us as a unit work, also. Still I am told that I am bipolar and schizoaffective. Perhaps I have more than one mental health gene that causes difficulty? Mom and Dad have spent more money on my health than it would have cost for me to go through medical school – someone should benefit.

One should be disturbed by the letters and essays in this chapter. I know I am tremendously. They bring back old memories of nights without sleep, empty gas tanks, and charred hot dogs. They bring back memories of being tied to a urine soaked bed, and given pills which you have no idea what they are. It is my writings which I have saved that keep all of this fresh in my mind.

In another letter at that time—which I will paraphrase now—I describe how it is such a hard way to not be in reality, especially to the distance of psychosis. Usually I am in mania and I do not feel the isolation, but that does not mean that tears do not come for long periods of time. Every minute is so very far apart. At these times many times people blame me for things I have not done -- others become angry with me and I do not know why. Most thoughts, situations, scenes and conversations I remember, but I find it difficult to really remember the emotions and feelings displayed about these things. It is hard to keep going in the end because I am so lonesome, yet what do I later seek? Yes, I ask to be alone so I do not receive more criticism from those I feel who meddle. It does not make sense half the time.

It is at this point that I become ashamed. How do I face the people whom I have talked with, interfaced with, and had strange thoughts in their presence? At one time I actually believed that Glinda was Gloria Estefan in street clothes. It goes even further when I believe that Gloria Estefan is a good witch. (And she may really be one) Pain and sickness are too much.

Whether or not Glinda has powers or not, why cannot Bob accept the fact that in truth there can be look-alikes in this world? Medicine and communication are both equally important. Things are changing again now that I am on Prolixin again. Sooner or later I'll get tardive dyskinesia and there will be more changes to face.

I tell the Lord what I want in my prayers. I want to live with a gentle woman as Leslie Jeanne and I do not want to lose the condo or car. But, so much can change in a relatively small amount of time so we will just have to be prepared for anything. Amen.

On writing about the food:

Good God!

Really, really-really-really-Really! I do not wish to eat piggies and moocows although I'll drink their milk. The reason is simply because pigs are more intelligent than most animals and cows have done so much for us already.

In reality though, if I was very, very hungry I would have to eat these animals. However I will be reminded of eating another mammal's flesh. They may make me eat it in the state hospital and I don't want to. When we come into a place like this one we are at the mercy of these assholes. As much as I want to pop their heads open and throw them against the walls – I simply cannot do that. "But, man, can I daydream".

I hate some people so much that I'd buy a ticket to watch them die. Hitler and Stalin come to mind. Get out of my life state hospital employees, especially doctors. Get Lost.

Go away Bob – no you don't.

Help us all Lord,

Bob

Now with some thought to more food:

Dear Lord:

This is not a holy fast. Instead it is a modification of diet. I will waiver for awhile but I am headed in a direction of less meat and more greens. I have taken nutrition courses at Penn – one of the best schools in the country. I take my vitamins plus medicine and know what to eat. I am a good cook. I do not like to eat pork, lamb or beef but understand that it is a necessity in our country. To help me remind myself of not eating meat I personify the names of animals, as a child would, so that I can feel the desperation of having to shed blood, give up milk and

38

experience the dismembering of bodies that goes on in every grocery store around this country.

"Moocows,"" Oink-piggys," and "Lamby-pi's" would do better near other species besides man. What if aliens came to this planet and did the same to mankind? Must man dominate to the point of decimating the world around him?

Good protein can come from plants. A little fat is necessary – yet all of this meat-fat is disgusting. Since diet modification means for now that I will eat some birds and/or fish then I will not totally be kosher. I keep this quiet for fear of ridicule and forced feedings of burnt meat. Also, for the time being I will eat what people put in front of me (with some rearranging of plate) as though I am ambassador of sorts to others. It has been known in some cultures to "do as the Romans do" when in precarious situations. I first did all of this last year before they all got together and put me in this hospital – now I want to do this more than ever.

I will for now eat chicken, turkey and fish including eggs. If I change in the future so be it. Actually there is an advantage to all of this because I can stay away from way too much meat fat. Yet with the eggs there seems to be a cholesterol problem – still have to watch that. I will find answers.

I feel there is real hope for products such as processed meat because it can be replaced by synthetic plant-made proteins. The key is to add nutrients, vitamins and enzymes plus taste. We could eat bologna that is not from a cow but still good protein. If man could do this we would not have the need to kill for bloody prime rib. We could dig deeper into the food chain as some whales do when they eat plankton. I would say that some of this type of thing is going on now even with the product Eggbeaters. That's the truth.

We stuff our fat livestock to death and then we give them hormones to make them even bigger. We stuff ourselves to what purpose? Is it a death wish? Unconsciously the girl sticks her finger down her throat as the matron "farts". All of us are reacting to the food.

All yours, Lord,

Bob

All the feelings, actions, and mindsets became clear once we saw the first clear construct about food in our culinary change in 1993:

We personified animals.

My wife and I kept returning to a pet store to grab on to good feelings as our relationship healed. We visited over and over an unsold miniature Vietnamese piglet. We actually watched it grow.

He kept running in circles showing off his black, white and pink coat. Since we kept returning, the pig got to know us and wagged his curly tail when we pet him. He would have made a good pet but we didn't have the space, time, or means to care for him.

Slowly at breakfast – even in the midst of our turmoil as we individually worked on ourselves – we talked of that pig fondly. Slowly our reconciliation began. We love mammals and cook no bacon in our kitchen. Thank you for another common denominator.

This we have offered to our lord. I have often felt that as humans see their gods as human, that pigs see gods as other pigs, and that kitty-cats see their gods as other kitty-cats. In other words the image of God is seen in different ways due to a special (species-all) perspective. This connection begs for respect.

Is now the time for mankind to consider how to treat the beings around him?

Is it also just as important to make changes gradually and not dramatically so to not cause strife? Let us look where we have come from.

History does repeat itself and the history in the books is not always accurate. We see what we want and choose to see sometimes what people choose to see for us. With great horror do I see and feel some things when psychotic but I am not violent. It's scary – as the movies I turned my head away as a child. Yet as a 17 year old I saw the murderous pictures right at the site of Dachau Germany. I hate those death camps. I *will* fight. I was in a death camp in a previous life.

Now I must focus on a previous life. The horror in this is the belief ['mental construct'] which I had for days in the state hospital about my own reincarnation. Thinking about it made me anxious, sad, and despairing. I wrote it down but told no one.

The following was a dream and/or past life:

> I was a king in a medieval castle. Some visitors arrived from France (we were in Germany) and we put them up for a few days. At a dirty medieval meal at night, food was brought to our long table. People brought fruit, chicken and other fowl. The people were so poor they couldn't supply beef. Instead the peasants have a roasted kid like cherub with an apple in its mouth. The French visitors wanted to eat it – Eat – yes, human flesh because this cherub was made to be fat so that it could be eaten. Some wanted to dig in and slice it with a knife. The main course looked too real. I was more angry than disgusted. I

40

called off the meal and buried the "kid" cherub with apple still intact in its mouth.

Later – a peasant came to kill me because he thought I ordered a cooked cherub. He did kill me. I was moved to the 20th century.

Now the anger comes out. I choose to use words rather than fists or sticks. I am disoriented and am not using logic but I am making connections much like this past history lesson. At one time I applied to be a member of the Secret Service to protect those they protect. My application was not taken – or rather it was taken but not used – Oh Well, I was not hired.

Piquing my interest in the U.S. government were chemicals that we students made in 1974 at Occidental College in Los Angeles. As an apprentice organic chemist under the supervision of a professor in the laboratory, I had to find someone to blame for these skin irritating, toxic and dangerous chemicals.

My resentment to George H. Bush is that he was Director of the CIA, and was moving to the State Department when I was in college. I made one of the chemicals, para-chloronitrobenzene, from one of these "recipes". This chemical could have been used by Iraq or Iran it was so potent, Bush knew this shit was going on. Included in his knowledge is the spraying of San Francisco and Chicago with other compounds which were being tested for toxicity. Go away, go away liar. Do not test U.S. citizens or cities with chemicals, radiation or anything else. Just go away!

There I was stuck in a mental hospital with my head in a fog about George Bush. It did not make sense to the present situation. Practically everything I thought about had no bearing on the reality of my life. I should have been more concerned about what I had to do to get out of this mental hospital. I was thinking of everything else but the most important thing - freedom.

I had a psychotic mindset at that time before entering the hospital where I felt aliens in time machines were making peace gestures by bringing Hitler and Stalin through time to a modern building in Moscow to let us torture the fallen leaders. You may remember in 1993 when tanks were shelling a multi-floored building in Moscow. On that day I dressed up like a doctor from the future and brought every pill in the house to administer to Hitler and Stalin. I would have liked to make them overdose on female hormones such as are in birth control pills however it became impossible to get a ticket to the Concorde.[Yes, people can overdose with any chemical if given enough of it – even with water. That would be called 'drowning'.] I really did need a doctor on that day.

The key in my psychosis is that I act on beliefs that are not true. Some of these beliefs are founded but not grounded in reality. Whether it is by doctors changing my medicine, or by not taking the medicine properly, my energy, agitation, and grandiosity go way up. At this point in my life I no longer feel embarrassment, but just a nagging ugliness.

This was the last straw that got me into the state hospital in 1993. It was in the fall and the Philadelphia Phillies were in the National League Playoff's. Although I did not go to the last game I showed up after the game and walked through their dugout and on to the field. All of the lights were on and the grounds crew remained to clean up the field. I was escorted off the field by two guards to talk with their supervisor.

"What are you doing on the field?" he said.

My quick response was well rehearsed, "I'm with a multi-national chemical company and I'm trying to develop a product that picks up bubblegum off of Astroturf." Admittedly my excuse was weak, but at the time it worked. At least I could go back to Delaware that evening even though later I was to be questioned by the Delaware State Police. Within a few days I was back in the state hospital.

Confusing as it may seem all of these behaviors, mental constructs, and mind sets went through my mind in a matter of days. It got to the point where I felt that each of them were completely true. Years before I had talked to a psychologist who encouraged me to "reality test" myself. But, I was so confused by all the 'stories' in my head that I did not know which to think about next. So I began writing only a couple at a time down for some future understanding.

Pathological psychosis happens to the vulnerable in times of passivity or aggression. This means that any emotion can be shown by those who are afflicted. More often than not the person becomes isolated and is either angry or docile. One cannot be certain of a particular reaction when approaching the psychotic, but generally speaking you do not have to expect violence. The isolation some mentally ill feel is a sad existence. Behind the laughter are tears.

Specifically for me, I have to state the reasons why I have become psychotic in my life. First, in the spring of 1974 at Occidental College while drinking alcohol I was tied face down to a bed and raped by approximately six young men. They would not stop until I 'played dead'. One person came and cut me loose. At that time any incident such as this was squelched by the college and no police were called [Or even came to interview me.] Out of denial for the incident I tried to continue my life. I tried to move onwards as if nothing had happened.

Second, in the summer of 1974 I went to my parent's home in Corpus Christi, Texas where I worked as a construction helper on the building of a plant that was to make fluorocarbons. At the same time other college students were hired and we all worked, drank, and tried other chemicals in the form of pills. All of this sped me into paranoia – a subsequent feeling which got me hospitalized. Later, after a semester off from Occidental, I went into treatment with a psychiatrist in Los Angeles who wrongfully gave me amphetamines in the form of "black beauties". Between the violence and the pills I had bouts with psychosis.

Finally, I have to say that through psychiatry over the course of 35 years I had become dependent on the major tranquilizers and phenothiazines given to me by the psychiatrists. We now know – which no psychiatrist ever told me – that use of these chemicals could actually change the neurons or more likely the structure of the brain. To get 'Off' these drugs would have to be done over years (instead of months) else one would fall back into mental psychosis once again. Four times psychiatrists took me off of this medicine too quickly, causing psychosis to return as well as hospitalization. I was only going backwards – having to take the major tranquilizers again – and never making headway. Whereas I believed the shrinks would help – they only proved that they did not have the answers either. When would anyone see what I needed? Why were the answers so simple, yet so far away?

In short, I was a rape victim who could not take the complexities of psychiatrist's drugs. Does any answer come after that statement? Yes – Post Traumatic Stress Disorder.

NINE

MORE ADVENTURES

This book is for those who are afraid to be called mentally ill, those who wish to cut the mentally ill out of their lives, and those who will care for the mentally ill. Its purpose is to dispel myths, affirm or disaffirm some generalizations, and educate. This writing is based on three years of my life on mental wards and countless efforts at recovery.

To illustrate a quality that always need to present let me describe a scene from a mental hospital. The quality here is not present, it is trust. This incident occurred in 1979 in a private mental institution.

The girl across the hall had cut marks up and down the inside of her arms. She had been a secretary up until this last one of her many suicide attempts (some were in fugue). By now, however, she was claiming success with her doctors because she had not cut herself in two months. As I walked by her room a male patient – one who had been friendly with me upon my arrival – stood by her door.

Suddenly he began yelling towards the staff, "Judy has cut herself – Quick, come quickly, Judy has cut herself again!"

I truly believed that I could help by walking into her room. As I went in I saw blood dripping on the floor from her left arm. She had opened a disposable razor and used the blade. I grabbed her arms and held on covering the bloody cut. She screamed.

When the staff members ran into her room they saw me holding her arms and I heard from the male patient, "Bob has cut Judy, Bob has a knife!" Even the staff believed I had cut her.

Not only was I duped but the girl was willing to cut herself to get me into a holy mess filled trouble spot. I could not trust other patients, the staff, nor could they trust me. It took a staff psychiatrist to get to the bottom of the disturbance. In the meantime I was tied up in the seclusion room. In the end, I could not even trust any altruistic instincts I might have. Life has changed since Eagle Scout days because everyone was a suspect. I cried in despair and was mocked by being called a "hero" by staff and patients. Only until later did apologies come.

People can go to great lengths to break trust. In the case it taught me a lesson to re-think the meaning of altruistic reaction. It made me wonder who I am. The event taught me not to meddle where blood and lives meet. My only answer is to trust myself. Others were concerned that I had created a crisis to take the role of a hero. In the end everyone felt badly except for my male patient 'friend'.

The moral of the story, "Don't expect comrades to come to your aid when you are helping".

Trust is essential in relationships and it is broken by one person putting their wants ahead of other's needs. (Not that I am solely a 'wants and needs' person). In my case, as with many others, if I cannot live up to the expectations put on me then I drag the other person down to my level. When it happens to two people at the same time the steaming anger is worse than watching a wrestling tournament.

Leslie Jeanne and I began truly dating in 1986. By 1988 we married in the Catholic Church by an Oblate of St. Frances de Sales. We went through matrimony preparation by our church and then double – checked ourselves by comparing notes on a compatibility survey. The survey implied that we would have to work on communication and acceptance of each other.

Since Dorothy, my Mother-in-law, has known me in 1987 she has seemed very intimidated by mental illness. She feels that it is 98% a behavior problem and 2% attitude problem. I also feel with some compunction, that when I talk about it near her she thinks I am making excuses for my life. With her Christian Science upbringing she feels that medicines really do nothing to affect the mentally ill. At an early time in our relationship, before Leslie Jeanne and I were even engaged I told Dorothy of my schizoaffective tendencies and how I was trying to overcome and recover from them. She never seemed impressed and, in fact, promised to never talk to me again should I bring up the subject. So as a result we ended up chit chatting about politics, cosmetics, and the fate of some species of frogs. We also chatted about the reality of what you could really see through a microscope. I knew she resented me and I knew she could not tolerate me.

Later when Leslie Jeanne and I were married for five years and Dorothy (my Mother-in-law) decided to cut us out from her life we had to face her again. Painfully, Leslie Jeanne was asked to come get all her letters she ever wrote to her Mother and painfully I was asked by Leslie Jeanne to come along. Her Mother was aware that we each consider ourselves mentally ill and that even our first date seven years before was to a regional mental health consumer conference. By this time Dorothy had plenty of time to be embarrassed and we had plenty of time to adjust.

We sat on her couch staring at one another. Dorothy began the conversation.

"Who do you think is better looking, Leslie or me?"

With a pause I looked at her and said "Mirror, Mirror, on the wall."

She replied, "Leslie is a real klutz".

"Oh I don't think so, "I said carefully". "Why do you always have to run her down?"

"I don't really mean it. I did not know I was doing that."

"To tell you the truth," and I could not believe I was saying this,

"You are not exactly the epitome of beauty." Here I was dragging her down to my level.

"Now look," Dorothy stated, "Look at her and look at me. Do you mean what you say?"

"Yes", I replied.

"Then you must mean it in some other way. Look, Leslie cheats with her diet. She doesn't eat meals and then she'll go and have cheesecake. What I and her sisters do is eat right and exercise. We do it the right way."

"I don't really care, Dorothy. Leslie Jeanne could be much heavier and I would still love her."

"Why are you Catholics all alike?" She said under her breath, pulling me even lower.

"It doesn't matter what you think," I thought to myself.

Much perceived pain has come from the thought of this. My gentle Leslie Jeanne was hurt and this was something I could not fix. It gave me more reason to want to irritate Dorothy, yet this could not be done for we were out of touch. Dorothy had cut us off.

So many people leave with a 'bite.' They have to hurt the other person when they leave instead of just saying "Good bye," "Farewell," or just fading from view. As a result much bitterness ensues. It's as though the one saying goodbye is disappointed with the effect they have had on the other, or that they did not get some reward that they were bargaining for in the relationship. In the case of the mentally ill perhaps the one that considers himself 'weller' does not meet his own expectations for fixing the other person. In Dorothy's case, I am positive she wanted her daughter to travel down the path that Dorothy would suggest 'to good' mental health. No doctors, no medicine, -- no outside interference.

About a year later I answered the phone at home to any angry, distraught woman. I did not know who it was on the other end of the phone. She demanded to talk to Leslie Jeanne. Yes, it was Dorothy. For some reason it was important to call Leslie Jeanne to see if she was still living with me. That was the last time I have ever directly talked to her and, once settled I was relieved. I do not work well on others expectations. Too often I end up protecting myself while not being able to be myself. Only by using forgiveness on myself and others can I come to a true understanding about the situation. It has always been my expectation that everyone should understand Bob. So instead of saying "Woe is me," I should be trying to understand the other person and use forgiveness. Truly, I must see the other person's point of view even to the extent of walking in their shoes for a distance. I must see the point of view of my Mother-in-law if I am ever going to get at the truth. The truth may not even be exactly how I looked at it.

Dorothy has always wanted boundaries and distance from me. She has wanted to be with her own friends and family and has kept me from getting too close by only socializing at the holidays and then moving out of town. For these reasons we have felt hurt and isolated. Only until later would I agree that good boundaries could prevent strong emotions from erupting. Distance provides a form of detachment allowing the individuals to grow on their own.

My relationships with Dorothy and Eric [(her grandson) (Leslie Jeanne's son)] have been telling throughout the years. Secretly I have wished for content, motivating, and productive relationships with these in-laws. Instead, the relationships have been difficult and I own my part of the blame.

Dorothy believed that if she backed off and gave us space – then Eric would grow to be satisfied with his life. She moved from Wilmington after we had been married five years. Her idea may have been the right thing. Unlike my family I believe my Mother-in-law knew the problem of faulty dependence in family relationships. People can flip-flop from becoming overly dependent on other family members, notably in financial, or decision making roles, to abruptly and rashly making decisions which affect the outcome of their lives.

This is why she moved away. I did not have the courage to match her lead. Only years later would Leslie and her Mother become able to tell each other that they loved each other. I am sorry for any role I've taken which could have wedged them apart. Too much quiet emotion had set our differences.

My part is that because of my debilitating illness I relied on my family way too much. I asked and let my parents help me when I should have made decisions about my future on my own. Yet I was also rendered helpless by the dependence on the psychiatrists and their medicine. I saw mercy coming from my original family and feared that I would not have the ability to be responsible in my life or to my family.

If people are going to cut each other off it would be wise to exhaust all possibilities of communication. It would be wise to keep lines open at all possible cost and it would be wise to have an adequate time of mutual sharing. A true sense of forgiveness is needed. I have always been one to believe that to maximize stability it is necessary to keep as many channels open as possible. Furthermore, when people take offense it is only a sign of an unmet need, and not necessarily a sign of rejection. A spirit of understanding is essential. Communication is the key. Just forgive.

In reality this is not always possible. I am resigned that I will not always get along with some people. In these cases its best to come to terms and move on. Some relationships are just not going to work out and they must come to closure. It may be this way for all parties concerned. I'll have to accept that fairy tale endings don't always come true.

In the next example I describe what happens when a doctor's trust is broken with their patient. I must use care, however, in the description of the treatment and medicine just in case someone else sincerely wants to try these experimental methods. What is bad for one person doesn't make it bad for all.

Precipitating change for me in 1992 was Dr Ozman who wanted to take me off of medicine I had taken for years and put me on an experimental medicine. Through the use of cursory exam – I held my hand up and he noticed how much it shook – he determined that I was getting tardive dyskinesia, an unwanted side effect condition. So he talked with my family to put me on Bozorine, ['Bozo' – rine] a new 'wondrous' drug that would cure me of my ills. Actually the media had touted Bozorine as the 'magic' for schizoaffective disorders and that the price for it would come down once more consumers caused the supply to go up.

Dr. Ozman, a private psychiatrist, sent me to the clinic where Dr. Ozite gave me another cursory exam. It was just like the military, they wanted bodies. I felt like I had been sold down the river. Now I had lost a private psychiatrist and had completely changed to a medicine where I had to have a blood test every week because of toxicity. I knew my veins were going to collapse after 52 blood tests a year and I agreed to this when no other treatment was tried for my shakes – or "tardive dyskinesia" (He could have had me take certain vitamins and get more exercise). There was also no evidence that Bozorine didn't cause tardive dyskinesia as well. There were no adequate explanations.

"Oh, you can quit your job," he said condescendingly. I'll see that you are taken care of," as he talked me into the experiment. With his attitude and that of the clinic I didn't feel like anyone cared about my concerns. It was at this point that I decided to take some action.

On their medicine I constantly felt tired so I took less than they prescribed. Soon I was spending nights in hotels and could barely function at work. Three other times in my life psychiatrists had changed or taken me off medicine and all three times I have landed in hospitals after horrendous escapades. This time I was coerced into the same scenario. [One other doctor illegally charged my insurance carrier before I had even arrived at the hospital]. Yet I did not want to be a non-compliant patient. It is fairly obvious that I am sick and tired of cure-all medicines from opportunistic doctors. I really do not want to need these people or their medicine.

I landed for a month in a private psychiatric hospital with Dr. Ozman as my psychiatrist. There was no sense of trust. He could not be sure I would take medicine and I could not be sure he would give me the correct medicine. Form previous experiences I know he was trying dump me on another doctor. He knew I did not want him as my doctor. By the end of the month our sessions had verbally gone in circles with no definitive actions taken. Then it happened; Dr. Ozman, upon my discharge told me to check into the state hospital and gave me nine (count them-nine) prescriptions to powerful psychotropic medicines. Whatever I had promised I knew when to take my leave. I went back to my apartment and went to the pharmacy to fill the prescriptions. With a warning of safety from the pharmacist they were all filled. I was free for a couple of days, maybe even a week.

The police picked me up in a hotel six days later. They brought me in handcuff's to face Dr. Ozman. Dr. Ozman did not want to face me so a nurse came out to identify me. She began crying because I described how I was left on a bed, tied up, and soaked in my own urine for hours in that hospital. She just walked into the next room and told Dr. Ozman that he would have to sign the commitment form himself. Sheepishly, he came out from a back office to see the police and commit me.

In my loudest voice I told the police about the nine prescriptions. I gave them the name of the pharmacist and the pharmacy phone number. They wrote it up and last I heard Dr. Ozman got a warning and a fine. I, on the other hand received the reputation of someone who doesn't take medicine and is violently uncooperative when it comes to treatment. This really makes me angry for now four times in my adult life doctors change or take me off medicine and then they blame me for the results.

Can't they see that they are fooling themselves? Can't they see that when they "tinker" with my medicine as adolescent boys with jalopies that they are doing a big disservice? My reputation comes from their ineptitude.

As it stands now I have left the private sector mental health care system. I am part of the public in a clinical-type setting in downtown Wilmington Delaware. I don't know what I will do if this new doctor upper handedly changes my medicine. By now, he should at least know this much. If I am going to work with a psychiatrist the rest of my life, I need to build something in the way of trust. I expect logical explanations instead of convenient coercion. The isolation I have felt as a mental patient has been tremendous. I have felt manipulation from peers, rejection and misunderstanding from some family members, and disregard from professionals. As a result I fight back and make others see that I want my way. It gets to the point where it seems like right and wrong have no meaning. I have struck my pillow and the wall in anger and frustration. At one time I was a decent human being now I am not so sure I want to be one.

It is not like the doctors weren't initially trying to help me. But I just hate their unctuous ways when they assume they can have me as a subject and not as an intelligent human being. They used no logic when dealing with me.

What happens when you are forced to watch out for yourself and you are not up to the task? What happens when action needs to be taken and there is no one to take it but you? What if you have to defend yourself? These are the questions I had to answer before telling the cops about the nine prescriptions Dr. Ozman gave me. His actions were wrong because I did not have a medical degree, and no one should be taking such strong medicine. I was also angry because he passed me off so easily to other doctors. I wanted a "bite" as strong as my "bark". In my last interview with Dr. Ozman he told me that no one would want to work with me because I had gone to the law so easily. Now I would get the reputation as a turncoat instead of working out differences with the psychiatrists. Communication, again, is needed.

Considering the dependency mental patients have on others, I understand their plight. They are expected to acquiesce to the wishes of doctors and family. Their peers do not stand up for them. All groups are snarling with their own agenda and there is no real refuge. Skills such as using patience and acceptance are not in the forefront. It becomes interesting to see these isolated individuals vacillate and have remorse while changing their minds. Therefore, decisions are made for the mentally ill and not by the mentally ill. All of this causes pain.

"Oh God, does it cause pain."

The issue of trust is involved here because of the mentally ill not being allowed to make their own decisions, and because of professionals and families getting swept up in the new treatment or medicine in vogue. Trust also enters in a personal level when psychiatrist and patient begin reporting each relationship. More information is necessary to insure caring relationships. Better communication is necessary.

In light of all three of the examples in this chapter it can be said that isolation occurs when one cannot trust peers, family, or professionals. I felt numb with anger when writing these examples. Even my fear was paralyzed and I felt as though I were walking into a concentration camp as an inmate. I could not believe it was directed towards "victims" of mental illness from other "victims" and family members. I could not believe that psychiatrists were so "book" oriented and so "people" deficient. I might as well be reincarnated as a lemming that walks into the sea. Don't I have a brain for some reason? Let's see if I can use it.

DOESN'T ANYONE CARE FOR ANYONE?

I want to take a strong moment here and say something of value. Dr. Ozman and Dr. Ozite are good decent, caring men. Mistakes happen and one can be a decent person despite therapeutic agendas – or even drug company agendas.

It would be a fatal mistake for me not to give others the benefit of the doubt. If my style is to complain out of bitchy, biting sarcasm – then I have to change. I have to know my part in the issue and in this case I have to know that I cannot expect everyone to be perfect for the sake of my self-righteousness. Any solution should come from the input of many. There has to be forgiveness else we fail.

Please let there be a check on my anger. If I say that it is "my way or the highway" – we certainly are *not* treading on higher ground. Anger dissipates in forgiving people when forgiving others. Love means that I have to share as well as accept the way others share love. I will still hold many people in high esteem whether they agree with me or not.

Whether my perception was right or not it was really true that for much of my young life I felt lonely. However, this feeling was only in my mind. While growing into middle age I did not fear the "Aloneness" that came with it, yet at younger ages I hurt tremendously.

For this reason, I have had a skewed view of my original family. I never would "own up" to my part – or role in the family. This meant that, as the youngest member of the family, I would 'Tyrannize" through weakness and receive special considerations for emotional gains. Yet, even this did not satisfy me, for with guidance, I learned that truly I only felt good when being useful to others.

You see me complain in this writing about being the recipient of someone else's babysitter, but you don't know that I am humbled.

People do take babysitting seriously. It is not just idle care from the older. Younger people see it as a responsibility. There are crowded classes at the YMCA of Delaware on how to become a responsible babysitter – many young people sign up for them. If Bob would look closer in life I am sure he would find many other good things.

Does the half empty glass still linger? I want to put a stop to my negative views on issues. I want to be part of a positive class of people who add to the good of society. It is important to know that Bob's negativity was changed to the strength to survive and live by the good in his original family.

"You may see this in other parts of this account," states Ted E. Bear. "Other perspectives are also shown."

"Why does he use us?" says Teribear

"For comic relief – just as Shakespeare uses witches, grave diggers, and Greek authors use a chorus."

"Don't give me that stuff," Ted E Bear continues, "We don't aspire to be in literature, at the least I hope not."

"Touché," comes from Teribear.

TEN

ATTEMPTS AT SUCCESS

I was born in December of 1952 and between my years of twenty to twenty-five became resigned to failure. Each individual defines his own stressors and mine were women, (girls) and work. For some reason none of the females, or work situations would last. It only showed that inordinate stress causes me to be ineffective as well as inefficient. I landed onto self pity which lasted for more than fifteen years and did me no good whatsoever. In these next few pages I will describe what it is like to live life as though the mainstream is passing – as though others see you as ineffectual and worthless.

For me, reaching a threshold where I finally admitted that I was mentally ill was disconcerting, yet easier than first thought. By age 24 I was over the hump and telling everyone under strict confidence that I was "schizophrenic". Not only could I get concern, mercy, and understanding, but I could have an excuse for any aberrant behavior. This is helpful especially at work. In a few cases it backfired and I was either laid off or asked to leave. Most people really don't have any idea what mental illness is all about let alone diagnosis it.

At about this time I recognized that periodic psychosis could be a regular visitor in my life. This scared me but I thought I could control it just with sheer willpower. I did not know if this was possible. I also felt I knew as much as any psychiatrist, especially about me and medicine, for none of them ever seemed to know anything. After all I was the one taking the medicine – I know how it felt and what it did for me. Psychiatrists just seemed like "bumps on a log" [as on an alligator] and really didn't do anything but add stress.

I must recognize that I have been diagnosed as manic depressive, bipolar, schizophrenic, and schizoaffective in my life. Things will be harder for me, and I will have to interface more often with the medical professions. It was the medical professionals who gave me all of these diagnoses and some professionals are better than others.

All I know is that by the age of twenty four I had three psychotic breaks in college and one in Connecticut after I left college. Furthermore, the one in Connecticut was clearly due to a psychiatrist who took me off all medicine just to see what would happen. I can trace three of my major psychotic breaks to doctors who "tinker" with my usual dosage of medicine. From what I can see the function of psychiatrist is to diagnose, prescribe, hospitalize, commit and reduce medicine. Northing else seems to matter to shrinks. Unfortunately, in my case, they like to juggle my medicine cabinet. If I had a long term relationship with a psychiatrist I should insist upon the same medicine that works, or else be committed over and over to a hospital. It should not be asked, but must be asked, --

"Are there incentives from hospitals or drug companies to change the medicine of healthy patients?" If there are then you can go to hell. A guinea pig I am not. "Go away; go away, I don't want you in my life anymore. All I need is the medicine, doctors, just go away!"

In later years the psychotic breaks were much farther apart. Both failures at work and relationship stress can add to making me psychotic. When a woman leaves me or when I am tremendously lonely then the episode is off and running. It has also been difficult going through life changes as shown in Gail Sheehy's, Passages or the writing of Erik Erikson. I have been known to work through younger stages at older ages. Right now, I am relatively stable.

As I write these words I feel certain tenseness about the psychotic past. I haven't been violent but appear and sound imposing when ill. I can remember all of my "Mindsets" – or what I had believed – when going through the psychoses. The thoughts are extensions of what a young or middle age man would feel, yet they are exaggerations and misconstrued ideas. For example when I was in my early twenties [the time for Erik Erikson's Identity Stage] I felt, like all homosexual men wanted to go to bed with me. I felt paranoid around men and feared any advance at all, even handshakes. Then in Erikson's Intimacy Stage I lost a girlfriend I could have loved and married. As a result I felt that women ruled the world and that the only function of men was to be subservient.

My pain was too much. It was clear that it was necessary to say that my psychosis was based on some simple feeling of reality -- but that it became complicated with thoughts and behavior that generalized outwards. For example, trying to kill Hitler and Stalin with birth control pills is not exactly reality. The thought of this, however, helped me lose some aggression. This particular psychotic mindset was a combination of aggressive feelings and a wish for hero feelings which I had three years ago.

A few years later a couple of young psychiatrists got my attention by telling me that there were schizophrenic and bipolar components to my history. I have psychosis with emotional cycles more so than the norm. Dr. Susan Poritsky and Dr. Kenneth Weller of the Institute of Pennsylvania Hospital had each told me that if I work on one defect the other would get better. That is to say that my entire condition would improve whether I worked on the schizophrenic aspect or the bipolar aspect of my condition. Cognitively speaking, if I worked to use logic to combat odd thinking, or if I disciplined myself during emotional swings I would then see improvement in my condition. Finally, there was a definitive from medical doctors.

Look closely at this next example and you will find a biological problem manifested as a mental problem. It involves a television report shown on WPVI which had been Channel 6abc in Philadelphia, Pennsylvania in 1994. The issue involved was goat therapy. As the reporter stated there was a humorous occurrence about a farmer's goats in Elkton, Maryland. Apparently, these tiny goats were a breed apart. Not only were they small in stature but they had a medical condition where their legs would become rigid if each goat in the family were startled or made afraid. As a result when surprising the goats from behind or by quickly jumping in front of them, the poor miniature goats would freeze in their tracks and fall over to tumble on the ground. Each individual in the family of goats stiffened and fell over time after time. This tendency had to be the result of a genetically inherited disease, disorder, or condition.

As some made jokes about the goats needing psychiatric help, the real truth dawned on me to the point of righteous discomfort. The goats do not need therapy from a goat psychiatrist. They need medicine in the form of goat neurotransmitters from a goat neurologist.

To be honest we must say that a component of both therapies is needed. In my case both approaches were needed as perfect medicine is so very hard to find. Therapy, even at its best, can never take the place of the right medicine. Unfortunately, the best medicines have not been discovered as of yet.

It should be said that the essential medicines have not yet been found. Exact molecular structures of chemicals are just not known yet. Perhaps a few chemicals are known like thyroxin, adrenaline, serotonin, dopamine and melanin, but are they specific to the human body and to what level do they have to be at?

Not only have the best medicines not been found but experimentation runs rampant. This is not always fair to the mental health consumer. Three separate occasions with three separate doctors, my medicine been abruptly changed causing me to become psychotic and hospitalized. Another time in the name of "science", one other group of doctors forced me into bogus treatment, which was called 'Orthomolecular Therapy'.

First, it should be noted that patients suffer when admitted to hospitals. They lose work and loved ones. They become confined and have to put up with condescending staff. It is especially tough is getting out of the hospital and building a new life. For me it has been expensive and painful, because of four doctors who experimented with schemes or medications. I have been through this too many times. No more. I'd rather see them suffer and I simply will not put up with this anymore. A lawsuit will be in order.

You say that I should find another doctor? In order for a psychiatrist to work for you he has to know you. How can you find a new one at moments notice when the one you have is demanding that you stop the medicine now or else there will be no treatment at all. Insurance companies are also no help at these times because they do not want to help in an unstable situation either. As a result, the patient is left to his own devices. What do you think happens on those occasions? Think about it. Does anyone have a responsibility? That's how I landed into 'Orthomolecular Therapy' in 1978.

Orthomolecular Psychiatry was actually a vitamin therapy used to treat schizophrenia. Actually it was an elaborate set-up to take money. Perhaps some day medicines will be found to eliminate bipolar and schizophrenic disorders but the technology just is not around yet. At a clinic on Long Island I was prescribed a regimen of vitamins after a glucose tolerance test. I was given an I.Q. test and told of doctor in south eastern Pennsylvania who I was to contact for further treatment. I was to continue my true medicine and take vast amounts of B complex vitamins, vitamins A and D, dolomite, and zinc. Dr. Bast was to supervise these meds – while he preyed I did not pray.

Things went will at first but after a couple of months Dr. Bast changed. He began showing me articles about a man who was perpetually drunk due to a special alcohol generating bacteria in his system. He told me to have only a couple of drinks a week. At this time I was fairly truthful about my drinking but really was drinking Fridays, Saturdays and Sunday's. Six weeks later he told me not to drink at all and gave me needles to inject a solution intramuscularly into my system. At this time my drinking increased due to the stresses of job and social life.

If he wanted me to go to AA he sure had a round about way of telling me. Other doctors could do it with so much ease and even make it seem palatable. Handing me a pile of IM syringes didn't do me much good either. I threw them at his door to which he said, "How crude!"

"Look who is talking!" I replied and walked out on him never to see him again. I had used Bast to the point of doing I.M. injections of *Candida albicans*, an organism found in dead people. Full of stress and shaking in fear it was necessary to find another psychiatrist right away. I needed the true phenothiazine medicine plus having the dilemma of how to keep a job, get the girl back, keep my sanity, and find a new shrink. This was too much to handle.

I'm not saying it is bad to take vitamins. I still take a moderate amount today. Five pills of zinc or dolomite four times a day is a little much. The whole business was overkill. The real issue was handing me syringes and having Doctor Bast say, "Why yes, Bob, we are trying to get the girl to return." You can tell that I was so well that I had a girlfriend I loved. The relationship went great until I became mentally sick in front of her parents. Orthomolecular Therapy did not work very well considering he reduced the major tranquilizer to my breaking point. I lost everything and ended up in a four month stay in the hospital. Truly there was no support. It was at this point that I felt like a mental patient.

Up until this point family had tried to keep my illness a secret, but now they were the ones who had to give the professionals my history. Medical professionals would not listen to my description of my own life. Something was gravely wrong – I was slowly relinquishing my pride until it was taken from me. Everything was too much to handle.

In 1980, after my four month stay in the hospital I entered nursing school to start a new career. The truth of the matter was that I was taking medicine regularly and drinking almost daily. Still the psychiatrists did not mention an alcohol rehabilitation center or question me on drinking. It only took about six months to end my career as a budding nurse. Whenever I did not take my phenothiazine I did become insane. This was true while drinking or not, proving that stopping the drink did not guarantee I wouldn't be put in a mental hospital. I take those medications to this day, for this time of my life I need them.

One of the real problems is that it actually can take years to successfully lower medicine instead of weeks. Many believe that you can stop it quickly but that only can cause dramatic psychotic side effects. Remember, if you are about to use this medicine, then you will need supervision during its withdrawal.

At one alcohol rehab I talked incessantly over the intercom while getting in all sorts of trouble (in psychosis) because "friends" told me not to take any medicine. I was transferred to another rehab which allowed the medicine. Progress was being made. I learned that I could take meds while not drinking or drugging. To this day, I am 43 now, and have not had alcohol for 13 years and street drugs before that (Marijuana is a street drug).

1981 brought new lows for me. As I was trying to get sober, I spent six months on the grounds of Crozer-Chester Medical Center in a psychiatric halfway house. I was the only person with a part-time job and a car. People treated me like shit. The house members wanted me to share the money I made, recovering alcoholics did not want me in meetings because I took the medicine, and administrators felt I should laize around with other members of the house. There were no friends, and the food was terrible.

As soon as I could I moved into Wilmington's YMCA and ended up in the Institute of Pennsylvania Hospital a few months later. One month later I went to live with the mentally challenged in Wilmington and living there I had my last drink and became familiar with friendly faces. Living with the mentally challenged was a challenge for me. Whenever my roommate, Sal, got mad at me he would unplug the refrigerator and I would have to clean up the mess. On the day I moved out to my new apartment again he did this, only this time he had to mop up the water. I just had to 'return the trick'.

These years I have just described were the toughest for me because I did not feel close to anyone. I was going nowhere, and there were no means available to better myself. I needed a future and solid advice. Instead people taught me how not to drink or use. That was to be much of my future. It was a miracle but it took me 25 months to stop drinking. I pray to God that it continues. By his time I was age 29 and I didn't have much experience in anything but not feeling well. People will kick you when you are down and it is necessary to be cautious. It was time to learn to respect myself and become stronger and wiser; by becoming 'numb' these things could be approached.

In this time, I had spent four days on the streets of Wilmington, crazy as hell, sleeping at the mission, and eating at a soup kitchen. I had felt the despair that many have and saw aggression in some faces. When I was walking the street, anger and fear enveloped me to the point of making my mind numb and my body sore, tired and weak. I felt as though people were looking at me with fear and distrust. It was as difficult to find somebody to talk with as it was to take a shower. Food was as difficult as getting medicine.

All of this is difficult to write, just as it was hard to live. Now I feel empty because I do not have a career or children of my own. But, compared to being "homeless", I am on the top shelf.

Life is vastly changed not because of the things in my life but because of the people. Before, I have discounted people. My parents or sister never seemed like peers. I did not want to associate with people in rehabs or hospitals. Even when I was young I was taught to have "sets" of friends. One "set" was for play, one for schoolwork and one for girls. I became too picky about my friends, now as an adult the parents are more equal, the wife is supreme, and the buddies are just buddies. I am comfortable with the present situation.

Somewhere in my unconscious I am telling myself that I will fall apart and die if Leslie Jeanne leaves me. I know isolation and rejection. I do not plan on committing suicide I just plan on dying. She is beautiful to me because together we are not made lonely – we are psychically attached. Slowly, warped past lives entwine together.

I recognize that people will go away in life. Eventually I will be alone at some time in the future and when death comes. The brain will die and dissolve. Thoughts may be separate and transmitted when the body is passes on. The body remains the vehicle for the soul.

Maybe I have wanted to die in the last couple of months. Maybe last year the spirit of Christmas kept me going. Maybe the emergence of a New Year keeps me from losing concentration and energy. But there has to be more than emptiness. I feel that some people see me inaccurately.

I am giving. I do care for others. I try to show my caring for others. Yet, Lord, I am also tired of humiliation and hurt, for it is time for a true humility. My basic problem is that I set a goal and fight to reach it but that it never comes to fruition. The problem is that I have desires but never make a habit of seeking. I have had goals but do not follow through on a daily basis. In order to be more successful I must seek continually, even if it means just a little everyday. It may be healthy to act like the fox in the Aesop's fable with the grapes; but does he every taste the grapes? Or perhaps I just was never given the opportunity to finish anything in young adulthood.

What has it left? Besides the empty feelings the lack of goal achievement has left me wanting to do something purely out of love. Getting through goals such as Eagle Scout or high SAT scores gives a certain satisfaction. It can be useful in the future as well, yet for most of my life I did not do things for the love of the doing. I set out for goals to put them on a resume, or to put feathers in my cap. Now, since I am not used to collecting laurel wreaths, I want to do it for desire. I wish to communicate to society the needs of many. I hope all people can be respected. I wish to love the process and not just the results.

Right now, I had desired to write about the emptiness felt in my preceding life. An emptiness that came out of illness and loneliness combined. This was an emptiness that seemed to never leave and one that was devoid of all sociability and spirituality. In reality this empty feeling was the result of an unsatisfying life where mental illness crept like cancer in putting walls up between me and others, with vain attempts at reaching out just for the sake of feeling better. I did not want to help others nor even want to attempt it. This went on for a number of years until I met Leslie. Before that I had just felt "numb".

Leslie is now the most important person in my life. Love is not stranger to us and we know we are blessed. Thank you, Lord.

I used to run by people and use others, chase women to conquest then try to gracefully leave. I've broken hearts and then after mine was broken I would try to break more. I was not caught and corralled by Leslie Jeanne – I just stopped. I stopped the chase and pursuit, I stopped easily going to bed and I stopped desiring a long term meaningful relationship. I became the bait on a fishing line looking only for friendship. So far this change has made for a ten year relationship which is one memorable in a lifetime. It is characterized by its closeness and openness. Rarely do we have petty jealousies or carry secrets from each other and so far during crisis we come together instead of moving apart. It's been that way since the beginning. For both of us, this is very satisfying.

What has not been satisfying in the years since my illness struck is when I get stressed with anxiety. When I am stressed my breathing becomes shallow, my legs get tight, and I want to walk. At this time I am either trying to control something I should not, or I have tremendous fear. Thinking all this over makes me depressed, irritable and angry. I can lose perspective and then receive an adrenalin rush that keeps me awake and up all night. In years past doctors medicated this insomnia but that always made me groggy, got me off my cycle, and caused me to want to drink. Now I just live with it and by living the best way I can -- sleep comes easier. Living in the presence of a compatible human also helps derive a better cycle.

I would sorely miss her if she had to leave --- but I would have to adjust.

As you can see, doctors and medicine can [but do not always] play a large role in keeping the mentally ill on the right track. Unfortunately in all cases the patient himself cannot know exactly what he needs, for initially the doctor prescribes the medicine. But with enough sensitivity and honesty it is possible for many mental health consumers to learn what is and what is not needed.

Furthermore, just because one sees a doctor (or any counselor for that matter) does not mean that one must "bare all" to that professional. Similarly, one should not have to follow the advice of others who will always disagree with your therapist. There is no need to discuss what goes on in a therapy room unless it is of breathtaking wonder or totally professionally unsound. For example to have "young bucks" tell me to get off my medicine is irresponsible. Those who think that treatment of a bipolar condition (and most other conditions) is a substitute for addiction are way off the mark.

Though gratitude is usually a conscious effort for me, the release out of the years of my twenties was highly welcomed. It took so long to find a new role in my family. Not only did Dad and Mom raise me from a baby to age twenty, but they raised me again from age twenty to forty. None of us welcomed this but it was done anyways. I gained a new role, and my family gained another son and brother. Leslie Jeanne gained a loving husband.

Finally, I must describe where I was spiritually in my twenties. I believed in "Something" but felt like any worship of it was obsolete. Rarely would I venture into the front door of a church and if I did it would be a self-conscious experience. Prayer was too much for me. Painfully celebrating Christmas and Easter was simply impossible. The biggest realization coming to me in my ten years of the twenties was to understand this statement, "Even if there is no God prayer is valuable. It works on the mind unconsciously, as self-hypnosis does also." That was my spirituality simply reduced to one statement.

ELEVEN

NOT ENOUGH

Teribear says, "How does one stay positive in all of this?"

Ted E. Bear answers. "Now his writing takes a new turn. One must at least look at the negative to capture the positive.

In mental hospitals and in the resulting recovery, people are caught up in a cyclical downturn of proportion that seems too much for them. It is necessary to be in reality yet be in optimism at the same time. This is difficult considering how people feel about the mentally ill and what lengths members of society (and even family) go to disassociate from the person in question. Instead of engaging in relationships – even though there may be no obligation - the mentally ill persons are left stranded because of an illness where they cannot adjust properly. Without learning a better way to have relationships how can anyone expect them to get well -- or even find a home in society.

As a result they are compared to either Patty Duke or Ted Kozinsky and must choose which one to imitate. Can't you see that it would be better to talk to the guy down the street and start a relationship with him instead of acting like some noted person on TV, stage or silver screen?

More communication between mentally ill persons (or consumers) is exactly what some government divisions want. The mingling of patients is needed so they can fight their own battles. In spots this is working and in other spots it is not – most likely due to lack of support. People laugh at you when you tell them that you belong to a mental health coalition. You are expected to play parlor games instead of litigate. Besides, it's obvious that some outside governmental figures want to guide things their way. Respect is just not present.

You Teribear, must see what we go through both in treatment and in our daily lives. From government to the hubris of the medical profession we are dominated. The living in the remainder of this book drives me into myself so I can rise again."

This is 1995 where I can say just what pleases me.

"Shit" I thought to myself. "I'm going to write what I want to write – no more, no less."

Who can stop me where I go? Today I went on a walk around the local suburbs and saw high school students playing touch football. As I walked through their street "field" they acknowledged my presence by stopping the game. I felt unusually self-conscious as time was spent before they could get on with the next play. The scene brought me back to when I was in high school.

"We get him on our side," one yelled.

I replied smiling, "Just go do a 'Down and Out." Only a few would know what I really meant, fully knowing that there may be more than one that may actually do a 'Down and Out' with their future lives. I felt unique with my past and did not really wish it on anyone.

In my high school days I seemed like a different person than now when I am more fortyish. Back then, I was outgoing and said hello to practically everyone. It was possible to remember names like never before, especially since becoming class president of over 600 students. People became a buffer, and if anything became disturbing, and there was a potential to seek advice or comfort from a wide variety of individuals, especially if I became embarrassed, self-conscious, or otherwise felt like people were talking behind my back. There was always someone I could run to if criticism was too much to bear, or if emotional difficulties arose. I was a social animal.

Now, I am just as self-conscious with not a tremendous amount of human consolation available. I am truly self-centered to the point of feeling that people – even the high school kids playing touch football – can see through me in all of my ugliness. Three years on and off in mental hospitals and constant cyclical "recovery's" mean that I have been ruined to the point of no return. Instead of doing well at my work, I have floated from job to job in a succession of failures. I even walk like I have a chip on my shoulders. Furthermore, I am stand-offish and reticent, and I over compensate because of low self-esteem. My illness has made me agoraphobic as I feel trapped on all sides. Family tells me to stay on Disability because they believe any stress will make me ill. Out of fear I follow their will.

I am pissed off. I am precisely on the line where going back to work could be much more detrimental than staying on Disability Insurance. Can't anyone see my dilemma? Won't anyone help in a decent way? I am a paranoid man who can't work.

Now let's take another look comparing and contrasting my early high school years to what it is like now.

First of all, I was traveling happily almost blithely, through early years where memories were gentle, warm and love abounded. Even the presence of love, food, sleep, and exercise was stable and consistent. Most importantly when I felt a disturbing emotion it was sublimated through work. I could work off my excess business and come to some sense of satisfaction. I look for the best and not for perfection.

Now, I travel with a sense of dissatisfaction, with memories of how people can be so harsh, and where emotionality brings a stoic sense of strength. In the case the deprivation of love also brings inner strength, no matter if the memories are of loneliness or anger. Something kept me resilient as an athlete after his event. Could he do it again? To

61

appreciate life does not always mean expending oneself over and over again at similar events. A true definition of insanity is doing the same thing over and over again and expecting different results.

An event occurred here. I learned from looking at my past and present that it is a combination of outside events and inner drives which shape my future. It is not always "being ready" for me to take on an event—it is being in shape in the first place that moves me to face the process.

I desire to be victorious, and this means that not only do I have to be prepared and be in shape, but that I have to be flexible and open while proceeding with caution. My advice to the players is "If you wish to be the best tight end possible then put a buttonhook in your down, run to the post and wave and scream. Get other involved in your life."

January of 1980 saw me deep in a private psychiatric ward. I was settling down in this private mental institution by getting to know other patients and by getting accustomed to routines. You know they have got you when you are more concerned about what goes on in the institution than in your life outside. At this point in time, I was concerned about the privileges of patients. It seemed that too many patients had been in the hospital for long periods of time, without even having the privileges to walk about the grounds. Staff was controlling the situation.

Privileges, or levels, as they are known in mental hospitals are instituted by the staff to let those patients who are trustworthy have more freedom than patients who have to be watched more closely. Usually, as a patient goes through his stay he rises in the ranks to a higher level. If, by chance, the staff feels he is not trustworthy or is caught breaking the rules he stays on a lower level.

Take Ray, for example. He was an average stature physically, remained quiet yet friendly, but always had to be escorted off the unit in groups instead of by himself. So instead of doing his beloved artwork off the unit, he did it on the unit. You could always tell when Ray was busy at work because the aroma of pipe tobacco that filled the room as he slaved over the object of expression.

Ray had been in the hospital for over a year. His parents were both doctors and that plus money kept him in the watchful eyes of nurses and aides. Innocently in his inappropriate way Ray was charming to me. He was well read, yet some people wondered if he knew what he was reading, because he almost always twisted everything around to sex or other mutually discernable hedonistic concerns. It was his lust that kept him going – especially in this "coed" young adult ward. Others respected him for his humor and longevity on this unit.

Bert also had been on the unit for a number of months, although he seemed more "with it." He wanted to be a lawyer. He envisioned himself as our "leader" on the unit.

Whenever there was a side to be taken or a peace to be had, Bert was in the conversation for what he was worth. He had this way of getting into other people's business and getting out with out a scratch – or so he thought. God did bless him with the ability to talk fast. It became obvious that his hysteria, when talking about his own issues, put him in the seclusion room at various times. Hell, he just couldn't take it. It was at these times I took pity on him but I did not want to show my feelings for fear that others would criticize me. Bert was popular in votes to represent us, but not by consensus.

Bert had come into the hospital six months after Ray and seven months before me. By the time I got there the pecking order by personality, as Bert put it and by length of stay was well established. Sometimes they contradicted themselves, but both Ray and Bert had their places, even though each one got on each others nerves at times. I noticed that they kept distance from each other. The unit had changed, especially now since Judy stopped cutting herself. Things were relatively calm and I hoped they would stay that way.

Then enters Jack; he was a little older than the rest of us on the young people's ward. He came in tight fitting blue jeans, western style black boots and Camels wrapped up in this T-shirt sleeve. With toothpick in his mouth, he talked quietly as the girls listened to his every word and eyed every muscle in his body. As he looked over the crowd, winking at a hapless schizophrenic girl, Jack braggingly stated that he was getting out of 9 months in prison for aggravated assault and that as a condition to his early release he must stay in the hospital for four months.

I could see Bert swallow hard when he came into our ward meeting. Not only would Bert have to make a good impression in front of Jack, but he would have to honor both pride and manhood at the same time. This soon became impossible once the rumors surfaced that Jack had rode with The Hell's Angels at an earlier part of his life. I never saw Bert so intimidated. It was time to be through with Bert as a leader and he knew it. Jack looked like our natural leader, he could replace Bert. I knew that Bert wished to be a leader but down deep he was "chicken". First of all, Bert acted ashamed about associating with others on the ward. Secondly, he was constantly trying to explain staff's position as though no one really knew how the head nurse felt. Third, the thought of having a tough guy on the unit secretly made him afraid. Change was in the air and he was afraid of confrontation.

It was time for one of our longwinded unit meetings and as I walked down the hall with Bert, Ray came up to us.

"Hey Bert," said Ray, "Have you seen the new man yet?"

"Yes, why do you ask?" said Bert haltingly.

"Just wondered, he seen you." Ray said

"What does that mean?" Bert replied.

"Well," with a dramatic pause, "I've been wondering something, Bert."

"What's that Ray?"

"You know that pecking order you've been talking about? I want to change it to something different--something very similar but different. It's called a 'pecker' order. Unfortunately, the girls can't get involved, but at least the guys can."

"Are you going to bring this up at the meeting?"

"Why, yes, but if I cannot bring it up before the meeting then I'll bring it up afterwards, if Dr. Tinman lets me."

"Thanks for letting me know," and then Bert walked on in front with a slight blush to his cheeks.

The meeting was long and arduous. A young woman complained that there was too much noise at bedtime. Someone else had misplaced a pair of tennis shoes and believed that someone had stolen them. Art supplies were left in a pile overnight and the cigarette lighter needed repair. Finally we received two lectures: One was, because of the heavy rains lately small rodents may be trying to make it indoors; the second was from a nurse on the 2nd shift saying that should a member of the opposite sex be in your room both of the patients would be subjected to loss of privileges. Finally the meeting seemed to be coming to a close.

Ray then said, "I have something. I guess I'll just show it to you." With that he unzipped his jeans, stood in the middle of the circle of patients and staff and showed his long flaccid penis to the crowd. As he slowly turned around to show everyone his penis, his eyes met the shocked Bert and he said,

"Well, what do you think?"

"Pull your pants up!" Bert shouted in a staccato voice "If you don't do it, then I will" and Bert walked over to Ray and was about to pull up his jeans.

"Hold it right there," Dr. Tinman said, "Who are you, to pull up his jeans? If he has something to say then let him say it. He wouldn't be doing this unless he has something to say. I know Ray. Bert, can you say that you know Ray better than me? Well, answer me?"

"I'm not going to answer."

"Yes, because you are too ashamed."

A hush came over the crowd as Bert backed away. I could tell he was feeling completely ashamed so I moved over to him and whispered, "Look Bert, where are we right now? Think about it. We are in a mental hospital. People outside these walls just cannot act like this. The laws are different inside than outside. Behavior like this is expected in a mental hospital."

"I guess you are right. I don't understand it. What is next?" Bert said nervously.

"Now, Ray, what is it that you wanted to say?" Dr. Tinman asked.

"Well, I have to say it with my pants down so to speak."

"Doesn't bother us," One of the women piped up.

"Me either" they all chimed in.

"What I want to say is this. When I came here there was much more freedom. People could sleep in more and I could leave my artwork in various places, the privileges were not as important. Now it has turned into more regimentation and control, and people's spirit is squashed." He was dangling now. "I'm not saying it is all Bert's fault or anyone else's for that matter. When he came to pull my pants up he was just being a pawn in the system. I'm just staging a protest first, by getting it to your attention and secondly, by asking you to join me."

One of the young women said, "What can I do to help you?"

"Well I thought if I could take my jeans off perhaps others could join me."

"Oh Ray!" another swooned

"What a waste of good penis." Jack said to me quietly. He apparently saw Ray with disdain.

"When God was handing out penis's he sure gave you a good one," Jack said to Ray.

"Thank you," Ray said, "Now will you join me Jack? Will anyone join me?"

Bert kept edging to the back of the room.

Dr. Tinman said, "I don't' think the girls should take their clothes off. Let's just make this a guy protest." All throughout the room were murmurings of approval and sighs of relief. The girls were all for the guys protesting. One guy in the corner kept looking inside his sweat pants to his groin and then darting his eyes to between Ray's legs and with a coy smile and a wink, shrugged his shoulders. Dr. Tinman had us all quiet down and he asked each of the males what they were going to do. The first to disrobe was Jack. He and Ray stood arm and arm rotating in a circle. The guy in sweatpants was next. I was sweating bullets, not exactly wishing that this group of people see my naked body, yet not wishing to spoil a good protest either.

Bert came to our rescue, "Dr. Tinman some of us will not take off our clothes, but we will gladly spend an hour in the quiet room as a sign of protest. You cannot make us take off our clothes." So that evening I spent an hour in the quiet room with Bert. Eight males took their pants off that night. Countless mentally ill women cheered.

The upshot of this protest was the privileges were granted to more people. Two byproducts were that the lounge area became more cluttered with debris, and Ray and Jack became more popular. Soon afterward the head nurse resigned, and a patient review board was allowed to interview and make recommendations as to the hiring of staff members.

Bert took things personally at first because he felt that Ray and Jack were teaching him to be less of a controller in a harsh way. But he got over it and turned out to be a pretty decent guy.

Dr. Tinman became an administrator at a state hospital one year later. As for me, I haven't been in a hospital in quite a while, but still heartily wait for a "Ladies Protest."

Ray and Jack did not have to wait for a "Ladies Protest" for in the ensuing weeks each was caught naked in young women's rooms. Jack was soon transferred to an alcohol and drug rehab something which Dr. Tinman felt he needed. Ray stayed in the hospital without privileges until well after I had been discharged. His art became more erotic and sexual. His methods and ways in the hospital remained the same as he became more predictable.

The moral of this story is that even in private and with permission there are costs to dropping your pants. Proceed cautiously.

Only a few members of a group can make the entire group look bad. This is particularly true in sight of sex and violence with the mentally ill. Whereas there was no violence in this case the sexuality seemed to move away from the spiritual and more to a power hungry animalistic world. Proper behavior was removed by a psychiatrist who ruled the unit dogmatically and patiently took advantage of this fact. Anyone looking toward higher senses has to search further.

Are we entitled to our present thoughts? Do we care what other people are thinking? Do we respect privacy? As the following words were written by me in 1997 do they have the same meaning now? The next few paragraphs show some of my wishes and observations of a 1997 Bob. In certain ways according to the doctors I am undoing stress through expression.

Private Thoughts:

One of my dreams should I ever become wealthy is to implode the patient's quarters at the state hospital. Of course, I wouldn't want to do this with any person in the buildings, but I sure would like to see them blown to bits in my lifetime. What a joy it would be to see those dilapidated old buildings fall.

As it is now, construction on the state hospital grounds is high, yet there has been no construction for patient living arrangements. The office workers and Division of Alcohol, Drug and Mental Health employees come first as far as space is concerned. All modern buildings on the state hospital grounds have been for people other than patients. Action must be taken now.

66

Imploding could work in a variety of ways – some which even may be therapeutic. All staff and patients could be evacuated to live in huge circus tents on the grounds. Tickets could be sold for the event, even to people all over the state. Chances on a raffle could be drawn to see what lucky person could push the button which would start the imploding cascade of brick, mortar, and steel.

Another possibility is to put all the patients in hotels throughout the city while staff brings needed supplies such as medicine and take-out food. Buses would take volunteers to the implosion unless, of course, the patients wanted to go golfing or mall-hopping. This guarantees choice in varying treatment plans.

Finally, politicians and state hospital administrators could keep mum about the upcoming event and sound alarms when action takes place. Then all the people would evacuate and the state hospital would be bombed silly by National Guard aircraft. All patients would then live in bomb shelters while ground is cleared and modern buildings are built.

If I were to pay for this implosion, then suggestions must be taken from a variety of sources so that the most up to date methods could be used. After all, how many holy edifices carrying the stench of a mud wrestler's locker room deserve to stand for so long? I feel that this is the only "blow-up" at the state hospital that we can afford to have.

Teribear says to Ted E. Bear, "It comes to a point where one must choose what to believe."

"What do you mean?" he said

"I mean do you use violence or peace?" she states emphatically

He thinks for a moment. "Yes, but it doesn't come by thought. When they take away all hope – then there is no logic."

She responds gently, "What you really need is to make room for loyalty, love, and communication in all families – even in the community."

"I have always prayed for something of that nature," Ted E Bear states plainly, "but I don't know if it is possible."

"You need more faith," she says.

TWELVE

AUTHORITY

As Dad and I walked, we talked. We must have walked thousands of times around these blocks, every night for a number of years. I'd be surprised if there weren't grooves in the pavement where our shoes rubbed. He so wanted to help me get another clean start in life. It was fall of 1996. We had walked after dinner and on weekends in his neighborhood for years. It was better than therapy.

Dad has a tremendous gift for listening. One those walks I would pour out my heart's plans and aspirations and make other plans for dealing with my documented mental illness. He would finally respond, unlike a therapist, by using his attempts to solve my problems. In later years when we would talk and walk he did not attempt to solve my problems but instead would tell stories from his life. Both styles worked. Spending time together creates a life long bond. Since I felt so vulnerable in the face of my illness I bonded with my parents in this way, giving up the notion that I would someday take off on my own. I'm sure these are advantages to both leaving your family or staying with them but in this case being a homeboy stuck with me. It was partially my choice.

When I was young my father was the authority figure even above my school teachers. The teachers were "rated" in my mind against the authority of my father. It was learned that if I moved close to these figures that I would get good grades among other benefits. So by using interest in the subject and a sense of humor I enhanced my grades until well into college. I became friendly with my high school chemistry teacher through the use of puns leveled at myself and my lab partner. We calculated joules (or "jewels") from laboratory experiments and applied them to our potential energy for having children. The teacher Mr. Toto would benignly smile and tell us boys to get back to work. He didn't mind a little levity. Dad wouldn't have minded either.

Mr. Munkie, the English teacher, was uptight and would only laugh at his own jokes. On my first assignment from him I enlisted the help of my Dad and wrote a paper that was very tight and succinct – using few words. In front of the class he made me admit that I used a word processor to write the paper. In truth, I did not know what a word processor was at that time, and assumed it was my father because Dad had me cut out many unnecessary works and phrases in that paper. I admitted to something I did not have. This first impression on Mr. Munkie affected how he looked at me for the rest of the year. I never received the grades I wanted in English and I respected Dad more than the teacher. This was my introduction to secondary school English and science. In college I chose to study science. Perhaps if I had a word processor, I would have studied English.

As I go through the years, I find that there are more authority figures than teachers and professors. Some may be counterfeit, but demand respect anyway. In the last few years one of these had to do with the law – that is police and a look alike. I cannot be certain if this man was a policeman or not, and I cringe thinking of the alternatives.

I always had trouble with cops because at times they could be rough and at times I was not always well. The last time they took a baton towards me. Leslie Jeanne and I were in our third floor apartment and I was wearing bathing trunks. We were talking on the balcony and along comes a middle age lone "cop" in a uniform and police car, who tells me to climb down the outside of the balcony to talk to him because I wasn't dressed properly. I told him that it was too dangerous to climb down and that I wouldn't do it. He shouted, "Then I'm coming up!"

He found the wrong apartment in our next door neighbor, scared the young woman by running a complete search, came to our apartment and pounded on the door. I showed him my bathing trunks but he still insisted on trying to "bring me in." This "cop" insisted that I was a john and that Leslie Jeanne worked out of the apartment. Even when we told him we were married he did not believe it. Soon he took his pistol out of the holster and he asked me to get on my knees.

"I'm staying right here in this chair," I said, "If you are going to shoot me then you'll have to do it to my face."

"I can't do that," he said.

"Then put your gun away. No one is in danger here. Not you, not her, and not me" said I firmly.

"What is that across the room?" he asked.

"It's only a bag of golf clubs," I replied.

"I'm going to take one," and with that the "cop" took my six iron, holstered his pistol and left. To this day I still do not have a six iron in my golf bag. To this day I cannot be sure if he was a real cop. I don't want to know either – I just want peace for my family. There were other instance with "cops" of which I won't mention.

Most cops are trained to a mode of questioning which seems to assume guilt before innocence for the one being questioned. I remember working at detox seven years ago and getting into what was seemingly and innocent conversation with a female cop which turned into a grilling of anything I could have ever done in the state of Delaware. Finally, a coworker who was married to a Delaware State Trooper told this female cop to lay off me. Finally she did. The "cop" from the balcony did not know how to ask questions. He was a counterfeit. I relate these stories to let you know that all authority figures are not what they seem. Be careful.

There are other stories and incidences which I've witnessed with cops but I am going to let them go for now. It suffices to say that police work is a tough business where all concerned have to look out for themselves. Don't you think its difficult being in a position of authority on today's streets? No wonder blunders occur now and then with stressed out individuals.

For the most part I show respect for authority. I almost get an adrenalin rush moving close to it or obeying its order. This has been true even since childhood. Yet with some people who are just plain mean, biased, or inconsistent, I care not to respect them, and try to ignore their authority. I have felt this way about some psychiatrists, clergy, bosses, teachers, and adults (especially in adolescence). I do not wish to obey and in short, just wish they would "go away." Some have to earn respect over time and some I have to "sustain with labor" throughout the course of our relationship. All of this can even be extrapolated to the media and its coverage of entertainment and politics. Why do you think I felt so strongly about George H. Bush at an earlier part of my life? Specifically, how I feel about the authority figures directly in my life influences how I feel about authority figures that are more distant.

Psychiatrists are directly in my life and they are a different breed. One of my early male psychiatrists asked me more than once to sit on his lap. He also said that he would "take care" of me. This made me distrust him completely and left me in a quandary about what to do. Trusting God-fearing people would not believe that a doctor would actually ask me to sit on his lap, and everyone else I told had little advice and kept their distance from me. I made my mistakes in my later years of college and needed just plain common sense. Now I am very wary of any one who tampers with my brain.

I suppose the shrinks are sick of me as well, after the fusses I put up about treatment. Somehow I believe that I am able to understand why and how the medicine works, and why they treat me as they do. Yes, I honestly feel that my mind is as good as theirs and I do not understand why treatment is not explained more often and is instead deemed to be considered "mysterious". It must be trade "secrets" for medicine is eclectic with science and borrows from it instead being part of it. After all isn't that why my last shrink handed me nine prescriptions when we last parted? He knows that he did not know which one I deserved. It must be remembered though, that one of the reasons they call these doctors "shrinks", is so my pride and "ego" will shrink as well; God willing.

The real reason why I don't care for therapists so much is because of their possessiveness (bitchiness), and patronizing behavior. Many times have I seen a psychiatrist get into my or someone else's life and demand to prevail in meddling with me. They really believe that 'What's good for the goose is good for the gander.' This first happened to me when I was told to stay away from my family. Why can't psychiatrists just "let go" and let the natural course of events occur instead of pushing and changing everything in such feeble human ways. Don't they even second guess themselves, or is their pride so strong that they must "tinker" with patients' lives ad nauseam?

My most favorite statement is "all I need is the medicine." I've made up my mind what I want out of life and I know where I hurt the most. If I need help working things through I'll go to a good counselor, psychologist or case manager. Psychiatrists are not trained enough to truly counsel even though their pride tells them they can do it. I mean it! I really feel my views should be respected. When it comes to *my* business it truly is the "caregivers" pride that is the enemy.

In conclusion, at least for thus far, the time spent with my Dad formed the model for what I think authority should be. If others do not live up to this model, then they don't get my respect. It should be noted however, that since I have lived with my Dad I recognize that he, too, is fallible and occasionally makes mistakes. Also, we do not see everything in the same way but nevertheless can work together well.

Two thoughts come to mind. First, I must realize that everyone has a tendency to think that deep in their heart they know they're right. Second, practically everyone deserves a good measure of respect. My higher authority is desired to be gentle and just, as I hope to be with others. Please Lord, don't let others mess with me and let me not get into other's business.

Purposely, I have let the clergy be last in the scheme of authority figures to look at because they are like the "grandparents" of the authority figures. Grandparents can get all the benefits of raising the children without really raising the grandchildren. Grandparents can turn the baby over to the mother or father when it needs changing and can sit down when the game gets too rough. Nevertheless they are authority figures just the same for their opinions are well taken.

I have witnessed psychiatrists complain about the clergy in a jealous sense because there was no theory behind what the clergy was telling their client. The particular psychiatrist in question spoke bitterly of how the priest was ruining his therapy by asking the client to pray for his mother when the shrink wanted no contact or thought whatsoever between client and mother.

Often it occurs in some doctor-clergy relationship that there is conflict. Doctors feel that they do all the daily work and a clergyman waltzes in once a week and ruins it. Actually, when you look at it, clergy persons do not have a strong hold on mental patients as the therapists do. As long as behavior is decent, as long as the 10 commandments are upheld, and as long as the patients care about the God of the clergy then things are in good stead. Compare this to the doctor who simply has to get them to take medicine, have good behavior, please the employer and family and generally take care of every other need before matriculation back into society. According to the shrinks there is too much to do and too many variables leading to failure. But the clergy, through God, seems to get more credit and the psychiatrists are left out on the lurch.

A psychiatrist who for a long time has been intellectually trying to convince a patient to always stay on his medicine is disheartened when he hears that God has convinced the patient to stay on the medicine "for now." He blames religion and the clergy for his client not making a stronger commitment to him, and he blames the religious for not being part of the treatment plan, but that brings on a whole set of other problems. Why do the clergy have so much power? Cannot two authorities work together? Is the pride of the therapist inordinate?

For the little weight the clergy have to carry in mental health, an awful lot of influence seems to go into the decision making of the patient or client. This is where the issue lies. It is not so much the religious worker on the mental ward that is causing the problem, or the chaplain in the major medical hospital. More likely it is a "friend" priest of the family who breezes in and influences the patient because the patient wants to see authority in someone else. This is only one way in which bad advice is passed on. Other means come with other ways.

"Turn me over, I need changing," the baby thinks to his grandparent. Now, when one gives themselves to another, all influence from other areas is nil. It means giving oneself to a doctor or priest with no in between. It means no compromise. I cannot go for that. A cult is not the answer.

Being naïve and being gullible are two different things. "Give to Caesar what is Caesar's, and to God what is God's," means to me to give my body, and that physical part of the brain to my doctor, while giving my living soul to God. In the end, they both will work together for the best. I only go to doctors who can work with clergy and I only go to clergy who can work with doctors.

It could be argued that my Dad on all those talking walks subverted the cause of the psychiatrists. He was not acting as clergy because he had an investment in me – I am his only son. Besides, he was a family member who had a pivotal role in supporting what was presented as "ameliorating" healing .Choice was ours. Succinctly put, we chose where the help would come from. Sometimes it worked and sometimes it did not. Many psychiatrists have yet to be able to pick and choose who they work with in patients. The entire system remains a bit nebulous. Authority once again seems pretty random.

Authority played out randomly, for me, at a very early age. Just as my father was a strong figure to me so was my mother a figure to my sister. Mother spent time with Annette teaching her how to organize and encouraging her to work at her talents. Now, Annette teaches grade school, is involved in a number of activities, and has three "children" graduating from college. One could say she is successful. My only claim to helping her with all of this is by being her "little" brother and letting her "practice" on me when were very young. Specifically, I am stating that it is intelligence and birth order which causes training and opportunity for one to successfully be in a position of authority.

Annette was six years old when I came into the world and she was able to learn how to care for a baby under the watchful eye of my mother. By the time she was thirteen she was able to babysit me for short periods of time. She became adept at getting me to do certain things as washing the hubcaps and bumpers of the car or picking up the dog dew before playing in the grass. Her leadership skill set was greater than what I could learn at the time.

Annette, like others, learned how to coerce through guilt, confront with animosity, or even plead in an assertive way. Directly I can say that I did not learn these methods until later in life and even still feel uncomfortable using them. I was a second born youngest and never really learned the skills of a first born. Things were done for me so I did not need the initiative. I had always felt uncomfortable "running the show" for a group of tenderfoot scouts, or little leaguers until later in life. As far as any authority goes, and as far as many first born goes, it is what you can get other people to do that makes you successful. This is true for a thirteen year old babysitter as well as the Chairman of Psychiatry at the local teaching hospital.

Many people in authority have had time to practice on others throughout their lives, and many people in authority are first born. The adaptations of behavior still astound me. For example I have witnessed doctors pleading with me much the same way my sister did when she was in high school. I have also witnessed doctors and nurses getting their ire up over the silliest of things and trying to "teach a lesson" to a patient who already knew the facts. This happened to me a few years ago when I was forced to take a medicine before going out on a pass from a hospital ward. Such a fuss was made to take the medicine, but all they had to do was ask. I would have taken the medicine anyway. It is not pleasant to be treated by someone else's babysitter.

Actually controlling people's behavior has been the history of America not to mention the world. First born and their kind have been doing it for centuries so why should psychiatrists be any different. Just let them heed a warning from me. Should their struggles over a patient ever harm that patient or anyone else I'd be happy to testify against them. It is more an observation than a major concern but psychiatric possessiveness over patients has got to stop. Learn to detach and if you can't then I'll send you to the psychiatric version of family court. Too much credit is taken by mortal men.

What about the rest of us? I am referring to those who are not first born or of the same stature. You can either learn what I mean by getting involved in dependent groups such as schools, scouts, day campers, geriatric homes, or teaching any talent that you may have. You may volunteer for any organization especially in leadership roles. Or you may study and practice. The object is to improve skills of getting people to do activity for you – some even call it leadership. I know a young man who went into the military when he received his diploma. He was told he would learn many useful skills but in truth he learned leadership. Virtually in every life, we can better our situation by learning or unlearning behavior that helps us associate with others in better ways. Learning the adapted behavior of rewarding someone with a pat on the back is light years ahead of whining and pining because you didn't get what you want. Who has more principle? The one who barks staccato demands or the people who learn how to put up with it? I would say that the principled ones can be followers, also, but it works best when all are principled – goals then are realized.

The struggle between authorities has cost many lives in the history of the world and has been implemented by many armaments. The struggle between psychological and psychiatric thought has also cost lives but has cost lives in a different nature. People are locked up. People are studied against their will or just plain unbeknownst to them they are examined. Psychiatrists coerce people into doing things they normally wouldn't do. Bastinda -- who can barely take care of herself -- talks excitedly to me about getting sterilized so she can have sexual intercourse with a male partner? Is this because a nurse mentioned it to her or did a psychiatrist order this? At the very least would the psychiatrist consult Bastinda's family, or guardians? Exactly how responsible is the psychiatrist to patients and family?

In today's mental ward and clinic it is this order which is hierarchy: psychiatrist, psychologist, licensed clinical social worker, registered nurse, case manager, and not the least, the aides.

Psychiatric aides are very helpful in maintaining the mood of the ward and keep track of the physical and mental activity of the patients. Case managers learn about the patients more in a clinical setting to help guide patients for living outside the hospital – other workers deal with social needs inside the hospital. The nurses are for direct treatment inside the hospital and administer to all medical needs of the patients.

Usually a nurse (RN) is the supervisor of the ward – a clinic is many times led by a Licensed Clinical Social Worker (LCSW) These people are trained for their work and have the ability to work as a team. The psychologist is paid and trained to know human behavior and its' aberrant cousins which come from dysfunction. They try to use psychology as a science and sometimes it really is not a science per se. Add the drugs that the psychiatrist can give to people and you have got quite a combination by any means. According to many professionals there is a treatment for any behavior or personality – but not all treatment will work on just anyone.

A contextual note:

As it stands now psychiatrists have the full responsibility for patient treatment. Not only do they receive information, feedback and results from staff & patients, but they make up their minds about which direction therapy should be taken. Treatment behaviors, as well as medicine, are ultimately decided by the psychiatrists. Responsibility is great for these medical doctors.

Should there be a slip up of ethics or in treatment the axe usually falls on anyone but the psychiatrist. He can blame others easier than they can blame him. Although the ultimate responsibility is his — others will lose their jobs first. For me this proves to be a nightmare for the patient. Once a person is in this system one has to get along with the psychiatrist — or at the least hope for compassion. I feel fear just writing these words because even a positive team can overlook something. At some time all people will make mistakes. At some point all patients will have to set their own course whether it be for independence or dependence. We must make a life decision.

It is important to know that there are well meaning, positively disciplined, good psychiatrists and professionals. I feel that all voices must be heard and that patients and clients must take an interest in their future. In other words everyone must move in concert towards a sustainable cause of health.

We all should also know that basic compounds, medicines, or drugs that are naturally occurring in the human body are needed to be discovered by researchers to aid patients. These chemicals would not just help people with mental illness but would also help give understanding to other disorders or illnesses such as ALS, Alzheimer's Disease, Multiple Sclerosis, Muscular Dystrophy, Parkinson's Disease, and other synaptic, nerve, brain and muscular disorders. Research should move where direction goes not just where the money surfaces.

All I can say to the physician is to please not make major changes in my medicine. As my clergyman once put it, "We all have pills to take: bitter or not."

When authority is assumed it becomes an illusion – when one grows into a position of authority gradually – the right touch has a better chance of appearing. You decide which authority to respect, which to coddle, and which to ignore. It is hoped in the end that the true source will influence with expression and strength.

Maybe I'll ask Dad to take a walk with me. There's got to be freedom somewhere.

More than everyone else I credit Dad, Mother, and my sister Annette for enabling me to quit tobacco and nicotine products. To you it may seem like a minor discipline, but to me it changed me more than I know and opened so many doors for me.

Up In the Air

The cigarettes hidden in the devil's cloak,
Will always lead to an early croak.

So if you want to fully quit,
It's necessary to bite the oral bit.

And make the habit of living pure,
By finally taking a breath filled cure.

Only after the healthy skill does float,
The memory's cleanliness comes by rote.

There really is no antidote,
From any tobacco not smoked.

So please do not use any nicotine,
The results, you see, are really quite mean.

Stop Please

With love,

Bob

THIRTEEN

RUDE AWAKENINGS

"Listen to me carefully," says Ted E. Bear. "For the book takes a different tact."

"You mean we've had only a partial view of the road to recovery?" says Teribear.

"Not only that," responds Ted E. Bear," but, Bob is hunting for something very basic to the core of his heart – a heart that had been changed by higher education, himself, and the psychiatrist. Now he is experimenting and taking more chances."

Teribear questions, "Is this book going to be about mental health or spirituality?"

"According to Bob there isn't much difference," Ted E. Bear states, "He tempts me to go on."

"From all appearances hope is removed and all that's left is sterile logic," says Teribear.

Ted E. Bear pontificates, "I have to explain a couple of things, Teribear. Bob wants healing and he believes it can come from a God of his understanding (or a God that understands him). Although Bob does not go all the way back to his past – he must look at the past. He must know his roots, be humble, and change qualities in current relationships. You do not know this, but it is life or death for him. He must look at himself differently; he must look at others differently, so a place in this world can be found. Bob has hope, but it is a quiet hope that counters desperation. His logic comes out slowly – but it is sound and strong."

The demure Teribear muses, "He is coming to grips with his statement in life – knowing who he really is; while at the same time knowing his limitations. That must be difficult for one who loved so strongly earlier in life. His limitations mean that he can only do so much in loving others. What happens next?"

This is a letter written about the time of my 1993 psychosis:

Dear God,

I no longer have a fear of death. At times I wonder about the circumstances of how it will happens to me and at times I may fear a fate worse than death, but once I get over the hump I do welcome death. This is part of my spiritual awakening.

The remainder of my life I hope to be useful in service to others. I also look for emotional balance with tolerance towards others and no fear of being alone. I will not fight the failures as I have in the past. I will try to be humble in ways I have not known. I will remember that every person has their story. I wish to be delivered to a new life making sure that I am prepared. The preparation occurs in this life.

Yours,

Bob

In the spring of 1994 I can distinctly remember writing that letter – with death as a new birth. I can distinctly recall my beliefs in reincarnation. In no way was I suicidal at that time. I think I was weary of the trials in my current life.

The truth of the matter was that except for a few fixating thoughts; my psychosis was not that bad. I could be talked out of seeing George H. Bush as an enemy. I could accept Glinda not being Gloria Estefan. My actions in the Phillies Veterans Stadium were not meant as serious, but as a joke. It's a shame to say this but good talking therapy could have prevented this mess in my life.

My fears centered about ridicule, and the upping of medicine which was certain to happen. The greatest fear was being locked up, a fate where no one could benefit least of all myself. Essays and letters written at this time do not come to any definitive conclusions for fear that the conclusions will land me for an extended stay at the state hospital. One letter is a description of a large purple mark on the right butt-cheek of a previous psychiatrist without once mentioning how I knew it was there. Another essay shows how natural selection causes mental illness in humans, yet goes no where in solving any problem except by saying that designer drugs will cure all ills. In short, I was on the run, waiting for police to come to my door and take me away at any time.

It was times like these when abstract ideas would console me. Abstract ideas are global thoughts that may be true. Dante wrote about heaven and hell. Reincarnation resurgence is welcome. Even terrifying stories by Franz Kafka can stimulate the imagination. Before entering the state hospital I found myself attracted to religion and spirituality, especially hyperbole doctrine and "wild" saints. Perhaps in a tamer sense this attraction has carried over until today. It should be noted that if one talks of "wild" religion or even of reincarnation that nurses and aides at the hospital will intently listen and furiously write. Also, most psychiatrists do not believe in the spiritual unless it can be used as a look into the psyche. Sorrowfully so, the little gods will agree with me.

Prayer

Lord,
Please let my words be understood for how I mean them to be,
Help me talk with healing instead of divisiveness.
Let my friends and relatives show me their love,
As I work to get it.
Finally, Lord, let me be productive in ways unknown.
Help us work together for a better world.

The perception of enemies, the feeling that we are closed in and banished, the need to be restored and the hatred of vileness make the mentally ill have this same feeling that the Old Testament Psalms describe. For me, it is easier to read the Psalms than the New Testament verses. Though I want this to change, I still pray to the Old God. Writing these words brings back many memories that I'd rather not have. The lack of confidence by family, friends and therapists make me angry and sad. The attitude of police and caregivers at hospitals I'd rather not see. In the end I hate to see the lack of trust that so quickly develops. It does happen though because people turn and no longer see me as consistent. I have to own up to my part. Even if shrinks have no need of God, I know that I need God.

By 1995 to pray or to talk to God became essential to me. Sometimes I would write the thoughts down, most of the time the words just flow in my head unspoken. Constant prayer is essential and I get better at it all the time. As I've said before, prayer is like self hypnosis getting in contact with God at the most. Sometimes a challenge comes and I have to think through it. Sometimes I have a spiteful hatred for others which has to leave as soon as possible. I have an older gentleman for a friend who always has to tell me, "Bob, think pleasant thoughts – just keep thinking pleasant thoughts." As honorable as that might sound it is very difficult to keep up. I didn't know if the negative spiteful thoughts are within me, come from outside cynical sources, or are due to the "downer" medicine I take, but they are troublesome and hurt the hell out of me. This is a constant struggle. Please release all hateful thoughts from me Lord.

When one is mentally ill it can take one little statement, phrase or observation that changes an entire mind set. When I read the following all of my religious thought stopped because I doubted faith. But the challenge was temporary simply because I just doubted faith for a short while. One small quote, one footnote can change how a person sees faith. In the library I looked at two-year old magazines. It was 1996.

Specifically, I have a quote from Barbara Thiering, Dead Sea Scrolls Interpreter, author of Jesus, The Apocalypse.

"It's in the scrolls if you really study the codes; it was not a resurrection. He was put on the cross. Those within his own party, trying to help him commit suicide gave him poison – the sponge dipped in vinegar. He was unconscious but not dead. His side was pierced, blood came out. A dead body does not bleed, so his followers knew he was not dead. They put him in the cave. He lived until his seventies, and it was he – Jesus acting behind Paul – who led their party out of Judaism and to Rome. He married Mary Magdalen and had four children." ['LIFE,' magazine, (Dec. 1994), pg80.]

Finally I have found something that makes sense about Jesus. Barbara Thiering keeps referring to his "party" as though it was a political party and indeed wasn't it as far reaching? Now, virtually one third of the world has heard of him and one fourth of the population of the present world attempts to follow his teachings.

Most likely he did do some confrontational teaching before he was crucified. Specifically I believe Jesus went to the temple and made enemies by becoming angry with the buyers and sellers of goods. He also made enemies with politicos by having the meek and humble follow him. They all helped him on the cross on that Passover day, that first Good Friday. Other miracles would happen as would other days in Christ's life but who could not respect a man who survived a crucifixion? True it was that Jesus Christ overcame death.

Why couldn't I figure this out sooner? Sometimes I can be dense. Something has always bothered me about the teachings. It makes one wonder about religious teachings – realism or psychotic thought?

He was doctored back to health and spent time on boats on a circuitous route to Rome. Jesus was a teacher, a messianic prophet, and a figurehead for a political party for justice. No one knows his true birthday and besides, it was on a thirteen month Jewish calendar at that. If I had ever heard any of this before, my religious upbringing put me into denial. The Holy Spirit coming to the apostles must have been a gathering of men who either witnessed or heard of Christ's cross trip. Doubting Thomas was more than one. All of the men learned new languages as fast as possible because they knew they would be traveling. In a sense it was the opposite of the Tower of Babel story in the Old Testament.

Now I will go to church to pick up scriptural clues. I'm sure deep in the Vatican the truth remains. I am too much a scientist to know that some of those stories are just too much, but I still remain sure that there are spirits in humans. It is important to stay away from superstition – it's scary, dangerous – and leads one astray. Beliefs, what are so important to me my sister can pass off by saying, "They are only beliefs, seems like every one of them is different for every individual." To me, thought and action follow from core beliefs. It is as though all one's actions in a day are built by certain basic beliefs. I cannot live by constant doing without inspirational belief embedded in my brain. Perhaps church will bring me more benefit than I thought. At least I can listen and make up my own mind.

All sorts of thoughts are now going through my mind. Stay healthy but seek God. This is the kind of material that mental constructs are made from. Why do institutions perpetuate myth? Do the myths consume the institution? Do the myths create more division than the religions themselves? Does practicing religion bring one back to a child's state of mind? Does it really matter to know what happened 2000 years ago? How else would we pass unifying traditions down? What is divinely inspired? How do we learn what we need to know? What information shall we use? Why shall we use that information? How can we insure aid to all generations?

81

I have talked to more than one psychiatrist who has said there is no logic in religion. I tend to disagree. There may not be logic in the emotional sentimentality or stories in Christmas and Easter, but there is value in perpetuating values, morals, and more.

As late as December of 2001, I found it very difficult to abandon all consoling thoughts surrounding the stories of Christ's life. When I read Barbara Thiering's interpretation I felt worse than when I could no longer believe in Santa Claus. I felt empty and betrayed. After my initial anger wore off it became necessary to do some more investigation. I call this "seeking God" and believe me it is necessary. The reason this search for God is so necessary is that it affects my mental health. At any other time of my life I could have been more anxious or taken off like Chicken Little and talked to everyone under the sun. I could have gone to the wrong people and be damaged by guilt, remorse, or anger leading to banishment from the church. This time I decided to do it the right way and to go slowly, not saying anything until the investigation was well under way.

The first place I went was to my local Catholic Church – to Mass to listen to scripture. There were some stories that could be interpreted in different ways and some that were quite definite, but for the most part there was always a meaning with a value or lesson. This includes those parables about mustard seeds as well as camels going through "the eye of the needle." Soon I found myself immersed in the Church, beyond what I wanted to be, in going to daily Mass, giving alms, and volunteering time. I wanted to believe all of the myths about Christmas and Easter. If I were to do this I would be denying and moving backwards – if I were to move forward I would have to ask for help.

Soon I found myself talking in a one on one conference with a priest. I told him about my logical thoughts versus my emotional desires to believe again as a younger me would. He thought for a while (making me wonder if he ever had these thoughts) and told me to pray to the Holy Spirit which I do until this day.

Actually all of this seems quite reasonable. I have been lifted to another level. I still believe that Christ is the Son of God but more so I see him as a man whose remains are still somewhere on earth. As long as I believe that Catholic sacraments are spiritually efficacious I remain in good stead.

Now what of other religions? Can they be explained to their questioning devotees as this one was to me? Do we have to get in arguments, fights, and wars over the nature of beliefs? I probably would have similar questions about the basics of Judaism or Islam or anyone of a number of religions if I were a member. I would be able to compromise doctrine to save lives, especially if the doctrine did not show anything to begin with, so I must look for similarities instead of differences.

One thing to pay close attention to is the value behind the doctrine. I wish I could describe this from another point to view than just Catholic, but behind all of the biblical Proverbs and Psalms is shown in this example:

Like an erudite, admittedly Francis de Sales writes with too many words in his descriptions of how to live a good decent life. In condensing the Saint's words Richard R. DeLillio makes six points about living in the present moment.

"Don't let the past drag you down. Develop short memories."

"Don't fear the future"

"Be a doer and not a worrier. Don't let boredom reign in life."

"Be appreciative; Show gratitude often."

"Overlook flaws ... see the big picture."

"Pick one virtue that you need now, and practice it."

(De Sales World newsletter – Fall – 1996)

All of this is part of Catholic doctrine but it gets lost in too many words in the original. This is good information that we can all benefit from. I'm sure other religions have similar nuggets. Why don't we look for them? These six points show a method which brings satisfaction in life.

Some people will read thus far and say that my beliefs are way off the mark. Others will be disappointed in me, but you can't say I am a man of little principle. I sought God and found an explanation, through a screen that filters the essential I am able to come up with a positive explanation as to what I should do next.

I will continue to find virtues in others and myself. I will stay in the reality of now by helping others where I can, working and writing to the best of my ability, and by showing gratitude for those who teach me. Finally I will finish this book on mental illness by describing what so many go through in their lives.

You can judge me by the mood I am in right now or you can judge me by the gloomy pictures I have described in previous chapters but it all remains the same – I am bipolar and I have found something that helps me. This time I won't let it slip away. I will keep my faith.

FOURTEEN

ANGELS

The pleasantly attractive young woman in the pew across the aisle from me was not the only reason why I attended daily Mass, although I cannot deny that she helped. Slowly, in 1995, over a period of months we became friendly and greeted each other with smiles. I never let her know that I was "investigating" the scriptures used in the church service but I assume she knew of my prayers for emotional balance and for loved ones.

In her greeting to me Glinda would silently wave at me and then wave near me to someone else. I always would turn to see that someone else but there was no one there – at least as far as I could see. Upon questioning her of this practice she informed me that she was saying hello to my Guardian Angel, which is something I never really considered. I can see the boys back at the state hospital now. It is necessary to protect people like Glinda from those jerks at any cost – or so I thought. It is more important to get my own thoughts in order. It is important for me to have faith in all spiritual forces.

In his book, <u>Angels, God's Secret Agents,</u> Bill Graham states; (1975, pg 74, Doubleday, Garden City, NY)

"We may not always be aware of the presence of angels. We cannot always predict how they will appear, but angels have been said to be our neighbors. Often they may be our companions without our being aware of their presence. We know little of their constant ministry."

My definition of an angel is any spiritual force or power that works for the good of mankind. When one feels an angel is near do not be concerned with the details – that is any classification system humans would devise about the spiritual world – just look for the good force. Remember that most major religions mention something about these spiritual forces or powers. Can something this definite and universal be all hallucination?

I am reminded of what a college professor once told me. He said, "At one time there were a number a cavemen living in a cave. Outside of their cave was a huge boulder which frightened them because of the shadows it cast. Not until one of the cavemen called it a 'Rock' did they all feel better. Then it was possible to talk freely about the 'Rock' and all its attributes and implications. Through man-made language a caveman can 'study' the world around him and we can study the stars."

Now what do we do with the spiritual world other than call in up-to-date "Ghostbusters." For this we need strong good spirits called angels. Although I believe in these good forces it is hard to say if they can be classified into nine the choirs or, Seraphim, Cherubim, and Thrones. To me an angel is an angel. It must be said however, that a personal guardian sure would be welcomed. Remember, just because man desires to quantify and qualify realms unknown does not diminish an angel's force. Good powers and forces are in this world that we cannot explain.

All beings are present for the love of God even though some have fallen dramatically. We as humans are not always capable of seeing this fact even though we try. Scientifically or even realistically we cannot prove the existence of the supernatural no matter how much documentation is used, but documentation is necessary. Even today there are periodicals which describe the supernatural such as the "Guidepost" magazine. With enough documentation a start can be made to at least list events which are strangely good and cannot be explained. Perhaps we cannot prove scientifically a good presence but enough listing of the unexplainable could make possible room for further study.

In periodicals such as these there is a listing of 12 to 14 stories of the good unexplained. Extraordinary events occur to people and they are reported. It should be noted that all of these events occur with some sort of intervention or guiding force or light – in some cases the embodiment of an animal or stranger person is used. I feel that never before has such a total documentation taken place. In fact the entire magazine is devoted to angels and its circulation goes to the public not just a select few.

Angels have been popular in past centuries and now for some reason they seem to be in vogue. There must be societal reasons why they are more popular with the public at certain times. For some reason I have always remained skeptical about any type of supernatural beings yet I know that I *want* to believe in these special friends that could possible help me and my loved ones. I know that when I totally desire for them to help me that they probably are busy doing something else. Then when I least expect it something happens that is more than fortuitous luck. I remain grateful and dumbfounded. For example I have driven all over this country and it has been 'luck' that has gotten me out of many bad accidents, but I do not want to act cocky and get into a bad accident because of inordinate pride. I remain a little superstitious about bragging. It's easier to assume that angels have helped in certain isolated points rather than take credit for safe bad driving. Sometimes you just have to hope that the other drivers are doing what they should. Angels help others too.

To me, it is the fight against randomness that the angels are engaged in. Total randomness on the road would have people driving up the off ramp and cars coming to a stop in the middle of the highway. It just does not work, so it is necessary to be organized in some fashion and perhaps that is what the angels see in us. Perhaps there is some supernatural organization which can parallel man's organization. We need more than time to see it. We need to be in contact with the spiritual world.

It is yet unfortunate that one cannot prove the existence of angels to me. I do have faith in the existence of spiritual forces which act as angels. I have not seen wings, or halos, or legions but they must exist. This is true because once an angel came to me in a dream and left me a message. Now I know what you are saying and I wondered it myself. "Of course a schizoaffective man would be visited by an angel in a dream. It's only natural." Nevertheless, the dream was so vivid that I had to accept it as real. Besides it helped more than me.

The angel said to me, "Reincarnation does make sense; in fact, some of us were human once. Someone you are very close with – your Mother – can be considered an apprentice for becoming an angel. Her life now is a preparation for life as an angel in the next. Amen." Mother, I know, does not like me writing about her and for this I have some fear in writing, but I will continue anyways.

Agnostic-Atheist Bertrand Russell failed to prove simple mathematical assumptions which have never been proven. I may not prove that my Mother will definitely become an angel and I will not even prove that there are angels, but I will show why I feel she could be an angel. In a sense this serves as a letter of recommendation.

Dear God,

Although Mother is proud she is also humble. She follows the will of God by judging the events of life through Jesus and through Mary – the Mother of Jesus. Mother follows through with daily devotions given to her by her church. She knew my needs after my last attempted suicide and took me to her favorite priest asking that I receive the Last Rites of Anointing of the Sick. The ceremony helped me because it relaxed me and made me want to be spiritually active.

I feel that Mother would make a good angel because she is thoughtful to others needs and considers your will. I have seen her go completely out of her way to help the poor, console the sick and love the unlovable. Her work is volunteering and she helps run a prayer line. She also has a strong will herself to accomplish tasks on behalf of others. This is shown by her dedication to her work at the hospital. She has been undoubtedly strong throughout the years by putting up with my criticism and retaining composure in the face of it. She loves talking to children and young adults.

I must say that she knows one of your legions but will not give the name of the angel. At times she has been known to talk to the angel. I recommend that Mother be considered to be part of your legion of angels, Lord, and in the humblest of my opinions I think you will be pleased. Just don't take her too soon.

Mother tends to worry but in a loving way. She worries about the welfare of people, about what food they are going to eat and about their safety. For all of this she will ask many questions, give away food, and pray for the well-being of others. She is too good to be human. I love her and for that reason I will not write anymore. Each angel has their own panorama – or view of the world. All accounts *are* miraculous but somewhat vague. My mother likes to be in the background, just as an angel. Please consider her for this position.

Very truly yours,

Bob

Knowingly I have never heard angels sing or recognized them as such. I have never talked with, touched or seen an angel. I believe in vast positive spiritual forces that can help mankind to each individual. I do not know if I have a guardian angel even though my Mother claims to have one. Since at one time I had seen the help she has received I have been known to pray to hers. Right now I am not going to worry why I cannot build a relationship with my own angel. Someday this will change. As late as early in this 21st century – after 9/11/2001 – I wonder just what I have done to others to cause them to react to me.

The horror of what has gone through my mind and how I have been treated by some other people on this earth makes me want to escape in dreams (sleeping or otherwise). Only one of these dreams has included an angel talking to me. I am still accurate in saying that I have not heard the voice of an angel or have seen an angel for a sleeping dreamlike state is not the same as living in the conscious. The only biblical reference that I know of in which an angel appeared in a dream to someone is Joseph the stepfather of Jesus when he considered divorcing Mary. It would seem that if an angel appears in a dream one would own the choice of the decision more. Just as Joseph made the decision to stay with Mary so I decide that there are good spiritual forces which may be called angels. As ridiculous as this may sound it was a big step for me which enhanced belief. Actually it is all a matter of perspective. Now at least I have turned the corner in believing that there are positive forces that maybe I can tap into while moving from basic pessimism to optimism.

Going back to Mother's Day in May of 1998, when Mom knew I loved her, I believed that I could prove something. I felt that if my mother was in this life for training to be an angel then there must be reincarnation of some sense. If you cannot believe this then just go along with me for awhile. Most discussions of reincarnation are moot, with neither opinion proving anything. Yet the Catholic Church remains politically in a stance of "No Opinion" concerning this issue which I take as promising sign. Just how reincarnation would work remains to be seen I have my ideas.

I feel that experiences, personalities, and pigeonholing all play a part in determining just what individual will be given what life. We are as a macramé weave with lives touching but each with its own end. A spiritual life may run the course of many lives and then end abruptly or just fade out. Isn't it conceivable that to have the magnificent minds of David, Einstein, Mozart, De Vinci, or Socrates (to mention a few) that many lives could have gone before? To unequivocally say "No" to this means that you are stuck as a mortal mass. Imagine believing that your entire life depends on a morality test that you take in the fifth grade. At the results of this test you will either burn or be in bliss until age 89. Is that fair? What purpose does it serve? Then you will be the same one who is either blessed or damned for all eternity due to a brief stay on earth. Who made up these rules? The body houses the spirit until the body does not function anymore. The spirit then moves – to another foundation if the foundation is strong enough. The only real question to be answered is "How long do spirits live?"

Depending upon personality, reactions, experience and what situation a person is in means just what type of life one will be assigned to in the future. A so called "good" life can lead to extraordinary acts from a "bad" life in the future. This does not mean that life is wasted by any account. A clergyman may not do as much good in his life as a gigolo who refuses to pass on the HIV virus in his life. (Do you really believe this?) A prostitute to a gang may be put in a situation where she could save more lives than a doctor. We cannot say what the macramé weave is in our life (or any other) – we can only be the best we can be at any given point in time. Let me sow you some possibilities.

A clergyman may return as a:

- policeman

- politician

- comedian

- gigolo

A hooker may have in a past life:

- hated men

- been abused

- died early at the hands of a violent rape

- been celibate until late in life.

A policeman may have a past life:

-where he has been a Scout leader

-or been on the bench

-or died a hero

-or raced cars

A scientist may have:

- been a farmer

- destroyed life until guilt stopped him

- hurt from disease

- loved someone who loved nature

A doctor may have been:

- a tireless laborer

- a judge

- a statistician

- a sculptor

A lawyer may have been:

-a cop killed in the line of duty

- an innocent aborted fetus

- a pacifist

- an apprentice to Robin Hood

If you are with me this far, then you can make up more of these. All you need to do is provide just one or two threads of personality or circumstance between the former life and the present life. Even if the life is a reaction to a past life as a nun and a prostitute can be considered. Whether a spirit can change sexes remains to be seen.

Today in 2003, many Catholics I know can see me as an anomaly. Here I go to church often yet when they see what I've written it is assumed I am a disbeliever. Nothing could be further from the truth. I believe as a Doubting Thomas would believe. That is it has to be proven for total belief, yet I carry faith with me all the time. I am sure that even a modicum of proof to Thomas made him a firm, faithful believer of Christ. Now after years of hell and three years in mental hospitals this POW is truly finding Jesus in his life.

One year later the adversity I face is the distrust of others. It first surfaced when I came to Delaware and because of the openness I had of someone from the West Coast some women thought I meant more harm than good. Delaware police have liked to question me about heinous acts I never would have thought of committing. Even people I thought were friends have questioned whether I was violent or not- or even should be violent. To tell you the truth I feel I could only be violent when defending a loved one. Really, I do not think I could be when defending myself. All of this is a great disappointment because whenever I go into a new situation I feel I am not trusted. Even now with a new pastor at church there is internal tension within me because I fear negative judgment. In reality, patience is needed and things take time.

It is not necessary to make a chronology out of this writing of all the negatives which have occurred to me over the years. I have faced adversity and survived and that is about it. Adversity has scarred me emotionally and spiritually. One cannot turn belief on and off again as a switch. It will take time to heal. Please, Lord, be patient with me. Also, please let me describe next in an understandable way what needs to be said.

Angels are just angels. The true focus should be on the Lord, my God. Angels are to God what Teddy Bears are to humans. That is their purpose is to support and console. I have heard of hospitals and disaster relief organizations that give out Teddy Bears in times of need or strife. At home Leslie Jeanne and I have five Teddy Bears each with its own name and each with its own look. This does not make us 'softies' but rather shows that we've had it hard. You could say that we have been abused or pushed around in life. The simile between Angels and God, and Teddy Bears and humans, does not go lightly considering that in the bear family are the most vicious and savage of creatures - the Grizzly bears.

Just as man can be in danger by these animals so God's world can be in danger by the opposite of Angels. It is at this point I will let the metaphor rest.

Life is a journey for everyone and for the most part we should respect other people. Only when I am in extreme pain do I not consider the other person. The road of faith can also be a journey and it begins with gratitude after a period of asking. I have mentioned that sisters and brothers in my faith do not understand what I feel, believe, and what I have come to understand. I realize that I am at the rudimentary level and that they may just be impatient as I have been with them.

I know that when push comes to shove that I revert back to my childhood impressions of faith. I pray to Jesus in the manger of Jesus on the cross. I kneel and hold my hands properly. Actually, all of these methods still work for me because they are reminders. Actually, I truly feel I can swallow it all someday like medicine good for the soul. You may ask, "Why are you putting up such a fuss?"

I reply, "With the complicated world in this day, one needs to fit it all together."

You may say, "But with my faith it all does fit together."

I say, "My density makes me keep looking and my experience keeps rolling along. To tell you the truth I am sure we will be on the same plane someday. Where you accept incrementally; I accept in large chunks. The understanding is the same."

Now my goal is to be a Teddy Bear giver instead of Teddy Bear recipient. As my faith evolves it evolves back to the teachings of the church. I want to love completely – to be consumed by love as Christ was on the cross. I wish to give to the downtrodden, to the people forgotten by the world.

Please, Lord, Help me love to the fullest. Lord, please take away any apostasy I have ever had. If I walk anywhere let it be towards you.

Teribear probes, "So Bob is going back to the church of his youth."

"For now he is but it is in a non-traditional way," states Ted E. Bear.

"If he does everything in the same way – he'll fall into the same routines," observes Teribear.

"No, something's changed, he may not believe in the same way. It can be said that because of transformation in him parts of his personality are 'rearranged'. The way he looks at himself is different. His belief systems have changed. Instead of feeling the center of attention all the time he just feels part of the whole," Ted E Bear says.

Teribear catches on, "So for someone who is not suppose to have all his faculties his *spirit* can make him well."

Ted E. Bear with glee, "Right – if one believes in miracles, then there can be miracles. That is how spirituality can be related to mental health. Just decide what you believe and keep it simple as you work towards it".

A brainstorming Teribear says, "I hear something else. Trust yourself and family (whoever you call family) and use discipline (whenever and whatever it is)."

Ted E. Bear continues, "Furthermore, Bob has learned to relax and 'go with the flow'. If it's worth doing he'll do it. He can only speak for himself though and even I cannot speak for him."

"What about all those people who have seen him in 'meetings' or church throughout the years? Can they speak for him?" Teribear then queries.

"No, they cannot," Ted E. Bear says, "Just as he cannot speak for them either. One's spiritual journey may see many faces, but in the end it is ours alone. For these reasons, the future is so difficult to see."

"You mean, I, as Jeanne's teddybear and you as Bob's teddybear will be on our own someday?"- languishes Teribear in wonder.

"Yes," states Ted E. Bear with the truth, "Even teddybears go their own way someday."

"Oh, my God!" they both cry in unison.

FIFTEEN

FAMILY

The writings in this chapter were written before 2001. Some were written right after my last hospitalization in 1993. i was pining and whiney. i was afraid and looking for strength. Not only was i afraid to venture outwards, but i had no anger for what i had let happen to me in life.

Now in 1995 i have to pause and take stock over what has been written. First of all my love and loyalty go to my wife Leslie Jeanne. She continues her work in nursing and has serious intentions on becoming a Catholic. For me this is a joy because we will be able to share the same faith and perhaps "bounce" off each other with spiritual messages. It is not difficult to be a Catholic because of the preponderance of churches and the ability to have daily social worship. Also, if there is any discrimination towards Catholics then we have each other and we have safety in numbers. Finally, in my life i am using routines to write on this computer and to discipline myself in my personal life. At one time there was something charming about being "young and dumb" but now i want to hone down to give to others a message from my life.

The message i give myself most of the time is "be prepared" and then get ready – a known Boy Scout Slogan. Actually for me there is no other way. For the juices in my cranium bathing my hypothalamus naturally can set me off into psychosis. i must be vigilant about taking the correct amount of – and correct medicine. Painfully everyday i need this reminder. With this discipline i gain my freedom.

Family and friends may give me the "warm fuzzies", but inner strength and fortitude come from mental and spiritual thought. For the longest time i believed that the educational system and psychiatric counseling together, without the help of any church, would help me, but they became sterile and there were no rewards. Now to add a church there are plenty of rewards and seeming opportunities to spiritually be part of the community. Spirituality is the umbrella for what i need.

Apostasy is the sin of walking away from your faith. At first i thought myself guilty of this in a bit by bit, incremental basis, but in reality there is a choice to be made. Slowly i forgot my roots via the overuse of hedonistic pleasures. When i went to college – 500 miles from the closest relative – i did not make one close friend in the new environment. i worked hard and played hard. Values became grades and grades became goals to obtain at any cost. i did not see results in prayer, searched for pleasure, and could not control life to my satisfaction. Then i graduated and lived on my own unsuccessfully and tried to be friendly with clergy while not taking part in services. Once hospitalized over and over, i interfaced with some psychiatrists who disliked clergy and churches. It was then that i turned from my faith.

i can remember feeling so self-conscious, awkward, and out of place whenever getting near a church. i had no idea what brought me to one in the first place and could not see that i was present for all the wrong reasons. At least now i can concentrate much better. [Parenthetically i should tell you that i am not for everyone being Catholic, or everyone becoming a member of our church, or even everyone being a member of the Church. i just want to heighten the consciousness that there is value in diversity.] The American Catholic Church could be a separate entity from the Roman Catholic Church. i was so twisted it was pitiful. Where some would say that i was twisted mentally without the church, others would say that i was twisted with it. The truth of the matter is that i want to be inspired and comforted. The spiritual is my last recovery. Early in 2001 I can see a direction.

The path out of my spiritual morass is hit or miss. For years on end i tried to work at trying to retain sanity so i would not go into hospitals. After a succession of unsuccessful attempts i became aware that a progression of events had to occur. It was not easy but i quit drinking. It was not easy but i got along better with my original family. It was not easy but i worked on maintaining long term relationships. Finally, i learned the value of good medicine. All of these successes came with the help of Powers greater than me whether they were from God, Jesus, angels, or saints. How do i know this?

The answers were obvious and in my gut. i knew these would work because they have worked for so many in the past. It was necessary to relax, imagine the outcome, not push, and take some confident steps forward. So many times before, i had grabbed on to the outcome with no regard to the process. Now i was working in rhythm and sync. What many people do not understand about the mentally ill is that erratic behavior and a change of mind are always possible. People do not understand how irrational fear can make behavior change in such a "flighty" way. At one moment a mentally ill person can be dancing on the dance floor and at the next they can be outside so shaky they cannot light their cigarette. This is true spiritual as well.

Therefore, by me "relaxing" back into the church i hope to prevent any "spiritual orgasm" in which the subject becomes an evangelist within a year and then is out on his heels the next. All that is needed is a little structure from the pastor and the realization from the individual that he is no different from the rest of the parishioners. i for one do not want to get off the deep end even though my mental religion has been twisted by my young adult life. Don't we all have strange ideas about life at one point or another?

93

One day after a daily mass Glinda had a talk with me. She was concerned that i was trying too hard to understand the mysteries in Christ's life. She was aware of what i had previously written about Christ and told me that if i could not believe, then at this point pray to some of the saints or the Blessed Mother. In truth, i may have been preoccupied but i was not in a quandary. It was true though on that day that i could not concentrate as well as usual.

Some outside the Catholic religion wonder why there are so many saints and people to pray about. They think we worship more figures than the Lord. Our answer is simple – prayer is just talking to a figure that can pass it on. The saints are many and varied because people are many and varied. Surely there must be an intercessor for you.

At any rate, Glinda felt i need to find a saint or figure in the church to help me understand Jesus better. Maybe she is right, yet this wouldn't be right to assume until i checked it out with our pastor or associate. Not only must direction come from the proper source, but i need to feel accepted by the local church and this may take time. There is simply so much information in this church that leaders must be cohesive and clear, and parishioners need to tolerate differences. To enter a parish is just like manufacturing a crisis in a mental hospital to see if one will get positive or negative attention. In this case though i am trying and putting hours of prayer and meditation into it – as much as i've put into my mental health-and for now at least that stands strong.

Maybe Glinda is right – i may be trying too hard. i ask you this: How can you believe or interpret a voluminous amount of doctrine or dogma that you are trained not to believe? This is what happened to me in my young adult life.

That day Glinda left me with two bible quotations. The first is from Philippians 4:13; "I can do all things through Christ who strengthens me." When i was a young man i truly thought i could do anything especially with God's strength but this was before i grew up to meet the world. i did not know my limitations – things which i should have known and kept track of as i matured. i needed to realize that to do some things i could not do others. i needed to realize there was a cost to everything. Too much and too strong were the winds of the world for one man to sail. i had to associate with others and i was either unwilling or unable to do so. Instead, i took daily medicine, exercised, and ate right hoping that was enough to stifle any dementia. It did not work.

Timothy 4:7 was the other quote that Glinda gave me. "i have fought the good fight to the end; i have run the race to the finish; i have kept the faith". This much is true, that i have done everything under my power to try and stay mentally sound throughout the years and due to the medical profession i continue to go in as a patient into hospitals. i gave up. i surrender to God. i pray to rid myself of the resentments that surface. i'm staying in this foxhole until they pull me out. Then they'll see a screaming man. Go Away! This is my foxhole and you are not welcome. Go away before someone gets hurt! Many isolated people feel this way not just some mentally ill. i am just a gregarious one.

i am going to have to forget Glinda for more reasons than me being a married man. She told me that she doesn't understand fully what i am telling her about myself. i admit i am one who says it and then goes on instead of rephrasing the same meaning over and over but to me that is no reason to not understand. Over and over i see misunderstood people as the object of ridicule or the butt of a joke and there is no one near who will save them. Then more often than not the people are criticized to the point where their ferret bites the offender in the ass and is shot cold dead causing tremendous sadness. Non-understanding snide remarks are just as bad. Change! Before the gentle see you.

Okay, i realize that everyone is in their own situation in life, but after i finish this chapter i am going to write about the stigma the mentally ill face everyday. It must be stopped. Glinda can wait for a long time. She is a nice young woman who will make others happy in the future. i am not meant for her.

After this diatribe and before the next i want to give you a picture of my faith – seriously. i listen to and like a large variety of music and much of it is religious or spiritual. There are two songs that sound out to me which really move me today. No, they are not "Amazing Grace", "Faith of Our Fathers" or "The Old Rugged Cross". They are not of that kind. When i really want to move and be spiritual I listen to "Jesus is Just Alright with Me" by the Doobie Brothers or "Spirit In the Sky" by Norman Greenbaum with the lyrics of "I've got a friend in Jesus." The heartbeat beat of rock music strikes a chord with my soul. Please Lord let this be acceptable.

There are things about my relationships which i find difficult and some of them have to do with my original family. Throughout the course of recent years i find my Mother, Dad, and sister sometimes distrustful of how well i have been doing. It has happened only once that Dad has let himself in to Leslie Jeanne and mine apartment without asking. i have been closely questioned with, "How are you really doing, Bob?" i have startled my Mother in fear by being at her bedside when she awoke from a nap after her knee operation. i had been an "intrusion". *That* made me feel like a real stranger, but i must give them the benefit of the doubt and assume they respect me. Even though i will never feel like we will be peers, i still have voting and squatting rights. Seriously, one of the best ways to control any trace of anger is to show respect. One has to work at respect if one is to love naturally. The bitter-sweet i want to convey to them is not from our lives interacting, but from my own life. Please let me find some value now in this 1997 winter.

Dear God,

Please let me treat the older generation properly,
With gentility, warmth, and kindness,
i don't want my words to hurt,
No matter how dependent, small, and weak i feel.

Let me treat those with bent and sore joints decently,
Lord, let me treat all of them decently.

Yours, Bob

The following are letters for Mother's Day and Father's Day:

Dear Lord,

Oh how should i write about my parents, dear Lord? Let me give them the benefit of any doubt. Please let me show sympathy to my Mother and hear what Dad has to say. They have stood by me for years, have loved and supportive me throughout my life. i never want to lose the memory of them. Whatever i've done for the good i couldn't have done it without them. Whether i am strong or helpless they are part of my life.

These parents have tried to be good and have led lives of positive example. Each is industrious, sensitive, loving, spiritual, and empathetic. Absolutely, their best quality is forgiveness. Over and over they bring me back to quiet "family times" where gentleness prevails. My life is so meaningful with them in it. Thank You.

Love, Bob

If only i could show my love with strength, in non-maudlin ways, then maybe i could be more proud of what i am. At this point false pride is an issue.

Dear Mother:

Mom, i love you. Sometimes i cannot always find these words but the feeling is there.

Please forgive me for i know at times i have hurt you. i know the reasons why. It's not the disappointment of not reaching my goals. It's not that you cannot be proud of me. The reason why i have hurt you at times is due to the resentments i have inside of me surrounding my own life failures. i have taken these out on you with my anger. For this i have deep sorrow.

Do you remember when i was a little boy and you used to come into my room at night and kneel by my bed telling stories and praying with me before i went to sleep? i looked forward to that so much. Perhaps i can do the same for you someday when you need it.

We get so involved in this life that we forget the essential elements of the next. i want you to have your blissful eternity. i want you to be happy and have peace of mind. i want the person inside of you to be satisfied. All my love, Bob

This letter to my Mother is sincere and honest. Purposely i left out most specifics because i wanted a generalized feeling where she could fill in detail from her memory. Stressing common feeling and emotion also helps. Being direct in statements help make it clear that i love her. For so long in our relationship she may have wondered if this were true. Just by writing this letter and knowing that she reads it eases my mind because in all honesty my behavior towards her has been off and on, callous and kind throughout the years. i never meant to be callous, but our emotional make up is similar while our reasoning is not. If i, therefore, saw something in her that i did not like but saw in myself, criticism would be directed at her. Peace does not come this way, but rather i should stress similarities instead of differences. Be good to Mother. Do not fool with her. Let her know i care.

i am running with the assumption that if i am as honest as i can be at any point in time, then i will learn to get well. i have to put up with these immature letters. Things must get written down and kept. A good truth will come in the end.

Dear Dad,

Remember when i told you that you were my best friend? Well, that was right after high school and now you still are. Just last month you told me that Mother and i were *your* best friends and i for one am proud of that fact.

Our family has what it takes to make all members satisfied. We may serve each other well. Granted, i have been a little slower than others, but there is a healthy respect for one another.

i am proud for you in your careers, Dad – both the one at the DuPont Company and now the one at AMID (Alliance for the Mentally Ill in Delaware). Unfortunately, i could not follow in your footsteps because i could not keep up the daily pace due to my constitution. Don't worry though, i get by just fine.

Thank you for letting your spirituality rub onto me. As i need it, this will continue. Remember, even though i do not look at things as you do all the time, your sincerity is the paragon of goodness. i am so glad i am your child.

Thanks for being you. It has meant so much to me and you are so special.

Love, Bob

What type of animal am i? If anyone knew it would be Dad for he has lived with me long enough. What have i written to Dad? This is a note on pride, respect, and example. Through our daily contact Dad knows i love him, therefore i do not need to send him a perfect letter.

Right now i want to call him to say i care.

Dad knows that i do some things better than he and he does other things better than i. My patience is beginning to match his as i get older. His energy is still high except that he channels into everyday by getting the same amount, and proper rest and food for each day. Daily we talk on the phone. Rarely do we have differences of opinion. Honestly, we are loyal to each other, but most of all i am his only son. Yes, he remains protective but not nearly as much. Three years ago i got out of the State Hospital and he was there to greet me. Just like other times and other hospitalizations he was there. i've changed and so has he. We are more tolerant of each other in that i am writing and working as i want and he is doing what he wants to do. Even if he thinks i am wasting my time, he respects me enough to not bitch at me to do more "substantial" work – whatever that may be.

Now, however, i should have to leave behind anyone – case manager, psychiatrist, Dad, anyone – who tells me not to do what my heart tells me to do. Strict logic and orderly direction do not always work and i will not live like that. My heart is in this writing (and some other pastimes) and absolutely no one is going to tell me to stop. If Dad could truly retire to some other love he world know what i mean. It's over for those who meddle with me. i love Dad but this is one falcon whose cord has been removed.

My feisty spirit of independence has been quite troublesome throughout the years. Every time i am mentally off kilter and am headed for a hospital i have wanted to be totally independent. It gets to the point where there is a "bite" from me to those i love. i want to make my own decisions independent of anyone else and sometimes i can get quite nasty. i the back of my mind i see just how dependent i have been on others and i react at my past actions in a negative way. In short, i am mad at myself for dependence and i take it out on loved ones. Family becomes my greatest foe and i painfully estrange myself from them.

The critical breakup occurs and i am alone again only to find myself misunderstood once again. Alone, i am in my thoughts. Reaching out occurs again only with time and when people are ready to answer. Each has to put up with the other's misconceptions. In a fragile way the communication starts again. Everything has changed. Usually i end up eating past words and painfully i have to accept the circumstances. Each time i feel like i am sucked into both my and your mental illness more and more. Independence is replaced by a feeling in my heart that secretly "i am right and you are wrong, but i will never tell you differently". Instead, you are beneath me and i hurt because i used you to get out of my prison. i, now, alone am in my thoughts. Only God can bring me a companion worthy of parity and equality. Are you the one? – i keep searching.

Family is comprised of people who have bonds with each other. i consider my friends as those who are one set of family. In the true sense of the word i do not "know" friends in quite the same way as i know my original family, but that does not mean i do not treat them in the same way. Usually i 'kid' hard in testing the friend and then i question if they really care for me when they 'kid' back. My aloneness consists of thoughts of whether i am being judged properly. i get tired though of always thinking about myself and use others to get out of myself by thinking of them in high school. i used to by pass the self-centered fear step and pray that i would always first think of the other person no matter what the cost. Now i just hope others do not notice if i first think of my needs. i am practicing and hope to be more adept at thinking of others. At least i am not paranoid these days.

Now in 1999 the third part of my family is the therapeutic set. This includes the doctor, administrator, case manager, nurse, and entire staff at the Continuous Treatment Team of which i am a client. i recognize that i should not put myself on an isolated island by having total criticism of the psychiatric staff. It hurts to talk about difficulties but honesty needs to be maintained. Should i be hospitalized again they would play an important role in my treatment and discharge. As it stands now they are playing a role in my maintenance treatment. For these reasons i call them "family," but as one may see i do not have much contact with them now. Once a month i see the psychiatrist for ten minutes. Each week i pick up medicine and see a case manager for ten minutes. Now, despite fourteen years of past psychotherapy, all i really need is medicine. Something must be working even though i am more and more alone.

Right now, the family is in equilibrium. Some are close and some are distant, but it is comfortable. Hopefully, if any changes occur – unforeseen or not – a state of flux will come present with some members becoming closer while others become distant. i cannot take an isolated feeling, or one where i am closed in. Balance is the key.

Live Teddy Bears are why i am living. Let's keep it that way.

LIVE TEDDY BEARS

Anchored in this family,

i stand from the inside looking out,

Remembering its frailties,

And infrequent inconsistencies,

Knowing that someday

All of this will pass.

Arming me to love,

What i once held in my grasp.

For isn't it the warm days gone by,

That makes all time fly by,

And the gentle, happy, times,

Which each of the present mimes?

Robert Franz

SIXTEEN

SPIRITUALITY

The word spirituality is from the root *spirit* – which is to infuse, animate, or encourage. It does not necessarily come from religion and has been credited to saving many a man. Specifically, it has saved this man during this lifetime and has left the knowledge that not all are "saved" in the same way. Some go to mosques and others temples. Some go to an assortment of faiths, persuasions or even AA or Al-non, but all can be "infused" with the spirit if they allow it.

In my particular case, as described herein, I state how I choose a particular religion and seek spirituality. A similar process for other mentally ill consumers when choosing a spiritual "hitching post" may benefit the cause of recovery in others. Now I just happen to be Roman Catholic.

My childhood days with the Roman Catholic Church were simple. I would go to church with family, be quiet for services, and come home and play. For me there was no pandering by pedophilic priests, no nuns slapping me on the knuckles, and no forced or coerced confessions. Perhaps this easy initial indoctrination is why I return to the church feeling a need.

Actually my spirituality is only partially influenced by the Catholic Church. For me, spirituality is separate from religion. This means that religion is only used as a vehicle to spirituality. Churches are man-made with divine spirituality coming now and then. Yes, inspiration from the Higher Power comes to the church at times but this only occurs at certain occasions.

All of this I did not think about as wine-sipping alter boy. At that age all I cared about was what girls my age would sprout up in nearby pews. Play was still important. There were times, however, during ethereal masses, when I hoped and truly prayed for a decent life. I would scrinch my eyes hard and hold my breath until I felt holy. I could pray better looking down at the floor not only praying for myself but for those in need.

To some prayer means nothing. To me I feel like I am becoming a better person. It is true that even if there is no God, prayer acts as a form of hypnosis and sometimes even behavior changes. God I must be getting better.

I never went to an organized catholic school in my life and instead went to Catholic Christian Doctrine (CCD) classes. This meant going to the church for one hour a week to learn about the faith. Lay people taught the courses, I may not have become aware of the essentials, but I did amass quite a few bits of information. This "schooling" lasted from first grade to tenth grade and included a group of students who became a community.

The root in the word "community" is the same as the root in "communion". Internally I would get worked up – almost an adrenaline rush – when receiving communion. I felt as though a bond was being created between myself and all those present at mass. Secondarily, I felt I could be a kinder and friendlier to all those I would come in contact with. It was taken to the extreme when my Mother caught me in grade school playing "Priest" with some stolen bread. I had learned everything except to have Jesus Christ into my life. This realization was made only one year before I knew what it meant to be drunk. In college I drank every weekend to excess, and wondered how I went to church on Sunday at college and couldn't concentrate at all in prayer.

During my "schooling" I could not believe some basic tenets. For example, did Jesus really die? Was Mary a virgin? Did lighting a candle enhance your prayer? Was the rosary too obsessive-compulsive? As you can see I was in trouble with my faith for approximately twenty years. I floated by avoiding church whenever possible and put on a show under the scrutiny of family members while leading a totally self centered existence. Rehashing this anymore is too much for me right now.

In 1990 my transformation began when working the night shift at detox. One winter morning, disillusioned and down on myself I decided to sit in the back of church just to see if I could gain anything from the service. I was struck that the lector was actually reading from the old and new testaments. At that time I instead found my message in the old testament of my Jerusalem Bible. It proved that wisdom could come from four thousand years old and still apply to current life.

> "Though you Israel, play the whore,
>
> There is no need for Judah to sin, too…"
>
> Hosea 4:15

Furthermore on a not too far off later citing it was read:

> "Grant us deliverance worthy of your wonderful deeds,
>
> Let your name win glory, Lord…"
>
> Daniel 3:43

I do not have to live like other people, I can stand up with strength using wisdom and ignoring idle wishes. With all my failures I can still be a decent human being.

Any type of transformation came slowly as I kept skipping weekend services but showed up at morning mass after work. I prayed for the healing of psychological illness in me and even tried to pray for others, but this remained impossible which meant that I was concentrating solely on my own problems at all times. The psalms with their paranoid flavor became my favorite prayer verses. There seemed to be an echelon of people who could pray well. Where mine came from a "foxhole"-- others were thanking and praising their God. Was this a style or does one mature to this point? I was so concerned about people thinking that I could hear "voices" it probably stifled prayer life. What about the ones that say life is full of constant prayer? I'm sure the psychologically minded would have an opinion. Frankly, I don't give a shit what *they* think?

These days in the early nineties I learned how to pray and then truly care about others. As I thought of others it changed how I pray. Although the center was on me I could reach out like branches came off the trunk of a tree to other people. I went to Catholic adult education to refresh myself with what I once knew and met new converts to the faith. It was refreshing to see people stand up for what they believe. My struggle was to understand certain tenets so I talked about this with my sister Annette. She told me that it really did not matter because everyone seemed to believe different ones. We all focused on different tenets or expressions of faith. Somehow, back in my mind I knew that certain specifics were needed to receive communion and I feared finding out what they were. In my case I was looking for a way into the church again and I had to know what to cherish and what was blasphemous or excommunicated. It was not just for religious or cultural reasons; I had to know for my spirituality.

I spoke with Reverend John Klevence of the Diocese of Wilmington, Delaware who agreed to ask me a series of questions which would determine if I could still be a Catholic even though I was baptized in the church. He told me that he would have to report his results to the pastor if they came out for the worst. He also told me that most likely (if I passed) that no one would have to know unless I told someone else.

"I have to ask you some questions if I am to help you," said Fr. Klevence.

"OK…I'm ready," said I.

"Do you renounce Satan and all his works?" said Father.

"Yes," I said, "Satan embodies evil and I renounce that."

"Do you believe that God forgives sins, that there is life everlasting and that there is a communion of saints?" said Father.

"Yes, I believe in those beliefs." I said.

"Do you believe in the Immaculate Conception, Virgin birth, and the Assumption of Mary?" He asked quite quickly.

"I'm sorry," I stammered,"But I just cannot believe those even though I try. If they all were true than Mary should be made as part of the Holy Trinity – which probably should be know as the 'Sacred Quartet' or something of that sort. Furthermore why don't we hear more of St. Joseph the (step) father of Jesus? Didn't he raise Him?"

"Bob, save your questions for later you're just suppose to answer 'yes' or 'no'," Fr. Klevence said.

Relieved he did not throw me out of the room I said, "Okay."

"Do you believe that Jesus Christ is God?" said Father.

"Yes, but he is human too."

"He took a human body."

"Do you believe he died and was buried and rose again?"

"I believe something miraculous and phenomenal happened, perhaps as you said, but something no one knows as truth. Yes, I believe that Jesus walked the earth after the crucifixion."

Father went into a different line of questioning, "Tell me about the Father, Son, and Holy Spirit."

"That would be the Holy Trinity. Each of them is God and as a whole, as one, they make up One God." I said sure of myself.

"Where does Grace come from?"

"Grace comes from the Holy Spirit."

Finally, Fr. Klevence spoke to me, "Do you believe that at communion Jesus Christ comes to us? Do you believe the bread and wine become the Body and Blood of our Lord Jesus Christ?"

"Yes, communion is sacred."

"That is enough for me," the Associate Pastor, "As long as you have been baptized you are a Catholic and no one can take it away from you. Furthermore, you think before responding which is something I do not usually see. You must feel the responsibility of having this religion as you feel a member of this church."

"Thank you, Father," I replied with relief.

It was all these words that make up the basics of my faith – no mottos or slogans like one finds in the Boy Scouts or Alcoholics Anonymous. For this reason I can say that I have another place to call home. They will even let a mental health consumer in. Now, I'm pleased.

I have the luxury, in 1998 of going to daily mass. The church rotates its biblical readings every three years so by now I have listened to the bulk of them. Some priests speak knowledgeably about scriptures and saints where others give no sermons at all. Either way the meanings soak in. All of this has added another dimension to my life by letting me meditate every morning in gentle privacy with highly arched ceilings. It does something to one's soul. I use the church and the church building to be hypnotized into a calmness that starts the day. Northing else quite approaches this feeling.

From a hysterical disease, one which makes me pace, stammer, and worry all over, I am released into a gentle serenity where I am aware of others, both past and present, which have lived and worked for the betterment of man.

Most places I go in these days I leave feeling slightly better. For so long I would abhor going to work or school – dragging through the day – only to rejoice when leaving. In church there does not have to be competition, reward, or what you think of earthy judgments such as with grades or pay scales. A diversity of people may attend daily mass. Poor or rich, dressed down or to be hilt, all are welcome. There is beauty in this religious service that has been going on now for about two millenniums. Every hour of the day there is a mass going on in the world – somewhere.

Some skeptical acquaintances will say that my prayers do not have enough faith. Others will say that I am not living the perfect serenity. No one is perfect and any amount of peccadilloes will not add up to a true sin. I am not in a race for the highest spirituality. Balance is necessary.

I try and I want to have faith not only to "get into heaven" but to find deliverance from the pain of mental illness. By trying, by praying I not only release myself -- with the help of God -- from the pain of mental illness, but I find faith as well. It is said in colloquial alcoholism recovery that if 51% of a person does not want to drink then they will not drink during any instance. As far as faith goes, if 51% of me holds onto the belief that Jesus arose from the dead, then he did. This takes time and prayer. Using a group's spirituality to enhance my own life's spirituality is inspiration to be healthy. It is a motivating force for mentally ill persons. By being attached and dependent we become free once again.

The religious spirituality is important to me because of the official formality associated with it. But there is also an everyday spirituality – a folk spirituality if you like – which touches us all and is handed down by word of mouth. The remainder of this chapter shows some of this comfort. This surrounds me in the late 1990's.

When my Teribear love tells her stories her eyes dance, smile, and twinkle across my face. She talks with innocence in a simple and proper way. Her eyes become windows to her soul which connect with me as though electricity is going through my body. I can feel a tingle start behind my neck and down my spine. Others cannot and do not reach me like Leslie Jeanne can. I am sentimental and begin to well up with tears.

My tears carry the vestiges of a frustrating cry from an infant, the painful tears of a toddler a lonely cry, an older more altruistic cry, and finally the sentimental bittersweet cry of an adult. Tears are tools of the spirit. They express strong emotions such as sadness, joy or even anger. Some of these emotions expressed are healthy and sincere and some of these are exaggerated helplessness. Sometimes one can begin crying out of altruism or identification and end up sobbing because of the events in one's life. Sometimes people just "carry on" because of their own life. Other times I can 'ball' in an ugly man-cry and not do it politely at all.

Tears are physical, mental, and spiritual spontaneity as manifested in humans. Recovering alcoholics describe sustained tears when drinking as a "crying jag". I suppose if I kept drinking I would have had many "jags" by now. But now my tears come on New Year's Eve when "Old Aung Sine" is sung, or at the ballgame, or theater. In these cases the tears are sometimes for what I've lost, but more often are for other people. The key is that now I do not have so much self-centered interest but that I am truly sensitively thinking of others.

Recently, in a popular crowded Wilmington restaurant, Leslie Jeanne talked to me about her work as a nurse's aide at a local retirement center. She is assigned to the older, more confused patients because she is good with them. In all innocence, Leslie Jeanne describes ninety-three year old Mildred to me:

"Mildred is the most cheerful, positive, lady I know. She likes the color green, and wants to wear her green blouse with her green lap shawl to every meal. She never complains or is belligerent and if she wants something she just repeats herself quietly so that those nearby can hear. To eat her meal Mildred needs her glasses – so she just repeats – 'Could someone please find my glasses? Could someone please find my glasses?'"

Leslie Jeanne turns her head gently for emphasis.

"Mildred," says Leslie Jeanne," Is sincerely happy with everything we do. She always compliments us for the food even when it is pureed."

Now I know from working in nursing homes what pureed food looks like. It is an absolute mess in all sorts of sickly pastel colors and to me is not appetizing at all. I also know that at mealtime there can be a lot of grumbling by patients.

Jeanne continued spontaneously," and Mildred said, "Oh this meat is so good – it's absolutely delicious," in a melodious voice.

It was then I knew something about Mildred. She tries to have a good attitude about life more so than I could say for myself. At this point I couldn't help it or take it anymore. Raising my hands to my face I sobbed. Yes, right there in the Charcoal Pit-Ice Cream Creations and all. I had not cried like that in public for over a year. It was a release.

Here was an elderly woman – stuck in a convalescent home – having a good attitude about pureed meat. Thoughts ran across my mind that Mildred may be trying to make friends. What will Leslie Jeanne do when she is that age? How about Mom and Dad and even my sister? On one hand Mildred stands out as a paragon of happy innocence and on the other as cheerful fortitude. Does anyone visit her? Is she really that happy and cheerful? Her spirit was too great for me because it is so difficult not to complain and maintain a good attitude.

"Well," I said, wiping away the tears," I wonder if they are going to puree our burgers here. What do you think?" My tears that came so quickly, left just as quickly. Mildred wouldn't have wanted me to cry anyways. God bless her.

Dear Lord,

Make what I do be worthwhile to some people in this world.

Help me show what I feel and believe.

Let people see me for what I can be,

And grant me the strength to be at my best.

Let me be temperate and kind with family and friends,

And let me be insightful to bring peace of mind to many.

Love, Bob

Honoring the elderly and other powerless groups is part of the value system of many societies, including ancient Native Americans and Israelites. At different times in history these two groups went from multi-theism to monotheism. Both were persecuted and both groups traveled in tribes. On the road to becoming modern society all of our forefathers and mothers had to walk through some of these stages. Strangely enough I feel that too many of the old values are lost in today's world. Our lives are so different because in a vast society people can feel isolated and lost.

Instinctually, mankind has traveled in small groups called clans, family or kinfolk. These usually number twenty to forty individuals that look out for the good of the group, and provide food, water, clothing, and shelter, as well as filling medicinal and spiritual needs. The entire group works together to help each individual in the group provided that the individual adds something – even if it is only by trying. For this people feel as part and are grateful. Rewards come to each individual by being part of the family just as each family finds reward from individuals. There is value.

In today's society people are many and families are sparse. This is true even if one uses the definition that "whoever you call your family is your family." People are becoming isolated from those who should be close. We take our children to day care, school and drop them off at activities. We shut away our old folks and ride alone in transportation machines. Some of us eat alone every night with prepared food. Others go to events with thousands of people and see no one they know. Still others marry or live together with no examples of partnership or stability from more mature family members. The young resent the older and the older do not understand the young. Communication is so bad because they don't spend time together. At some point in time everyone is miserable and too many have thought of suicide. My life is no different.

I come from an original family of four and at this point now I am alone with Leslie Jeanne. I have "family" in Wilmington in the form of friends and acquaintances but most of these are very transient in my life. We do not travel with blood or adopted clan members. There is no house full of kin, to say the least. Who do we know on group health insurance? Neither Leslie Jeanne nor I have more than three relatives who we can rely on nearby. My relatives are in San Diego, San Jose, Davis, Indiana, West Virginia, Louisiana, Wilmington and God knows where else. Leslie Jeanne's are in Minnesota, Florida, Kentucky and Indiana. It has gotten to the point that in our country it is described by one of my Dad's friends just perfectly, "After leaving my son in California and two daughters in different parts of Texas I came to Wilmington feeling like a she-bitch dog having puppies in different parts of the country." Where is the continuity? Where is the community? Let me explain my greatest loss.

Whether religious or scientific, the reality is that at some point in time the human race "traveled" in clans. In modern day life this is disappearing and it is hurting society. The summer I left my hometown and into the fall when I knew I would never return, was pivotal in bringing stress on me. I needed people who knew me and all I was given were strangers. Even now I feel the isolation of not having relatives near. My life is full of strangers.

It is my theory that I have a genetic predisposition towards mental illness. It doesn't take much more to say that this mental illness drove me to drink like an alcoholic and live a reckless life. Psychotic thought became real at stressful points and I was hospitalized. Always, during the drinking times or times of psychosis I was isolated physically, mentally, emotionally, or spiritually. There was not enough contact with relatives. I was given the space a mass murderer would receive. I needed my tribe. Where were my people? For me only the relative would do. Where were they? To stigmatize you have to isolate. To isolate means to become highly neurotic or psychotic. I became the latter.

I'll make a wager with you that if I had family helping me (I mean a clan or extended family) then I would have learned how to "deal" sooner and would not have faced so much. Ideally I may have never had the illness at all if I was raised with family. If wishes were ferrets, I'd be soft and cuddly now and perfect in all ways. No one can stop the reality of now.

Throughout this writing I have mentioned people who at the time have meant something to me. Now I write letters to some of those whom I consider as my close family, in part to tell you – the reader – not only who they are but what topics I am trying to stress in this manuscript.

"Sometimes the closest teddybears can see all that I am made from – even my stuffing," says Ted E. Bear.

"Do we dare to care?" replies Teribear "I must tell the truth to those I love. I must overlook the shortcomings of others and still continue to see moments of understanding. If we can work on the details *and* see the big picture of thankfulness then life becomes more rewarding."

SEVENTEEN

SENTIMENTS

I want to show my appreciation for six close relationships that have affected our married life much for the positive. They have kept me acting stable; they have kept us in equilibrium. Specifically I want to write about each one and then through letters to these people do I want to show you just what I want to say to them. I am including these letters because I feel you are watching me relating to those who I feel have been so valuable.

Ernie was my father-in-law who loved to apply science and could be very impetuous. As Leslie's father he tried to be open to many new ideas and he was very supportive. Although he could be protective he was not necessarily a disciplinarian. He cared deeply for his grandson Eric as he tried to lay the groundwork based on his chemical doctorate training. I cared for him because he seemed to know what love was and because loyally he cared for all of his family. When he passed in 2010 we all were sad. Just for me, I was impressed that he always talked adult to adult with me and offered encouragement even if I was not thinking right. I thank him for having confidence in me. When he knew I was trying to quit smoking all tobacco products, Ernie kept telling me," Bob, I know you are going to quit someday – I just know you are!" Ernie boosted the confidence of others.

I am sure that Ernie would have moved back to Wilmington, Delaware if it were at all possible. Business kept my in-laws apart. Here shown is a letter I sent Ernie in the summer of 1996. It went to the town of New Albany, Indiana.

Dear Ernie,

Writing is such an arduous task but nevertheless I enjoy it. I just wish that someone would read it and enjoy it as I have written. I hope you see my problem behind this manuscript – which is mental illness. I have described it the best way I know how seeing that only the written word is more permanent than the spoken word. My primary objective is not to be literary but to have a record for medical practitioners whose job it is to treat me. It's odd, but I fear that criticism of the English crowd – professors and the like. Still, I feel I can stand up to the psychologist and psychiatrists who may take a peek.

I remember fairly well in 1993 when I talked to you from Wilmington to Indiana over the phone. You were one of the only people who would talk to me decently considering that I had such strange mental constructs and mind sets. I really appreciate it. Let's keep up regular communications.

Ernie, please consider moving hack to Wilmington. I say this because it would really mean a lot to Jeanne and Eric. I think it would mean something to all of us. I know you give me credit for "raising" Eric, for part of his life, but you don't realize that when Leslie Jeanne and I were married Eric was already fifteen. He may have been happy to receive another "parent" but his rearing had been done. Truly I feel you would not be over taxed by this and you may get some rewards. I am sure they are for it, so please consider this.

Finally, thank you so much for walking down the aisle and giving your blessing to Leslie Jeanne and me at our wedding. She means so much to me and is always full of support. I don't feel you know of the fond memories she (and I) have to you.

Ernie, whether it's talking about a monotheistic God, discussing the life of early man, or just walking on the beach I want you know we care for you.

Say hello and give our love to Ruth for us.

Love, Bob

I met Ernie and Eric, my son (stepson), in the fall of 1986. When Leslie and I made more permanent plans it became very important to see how Eric felt about us and life in general. At the age of thirteen Eric was gaining on some definite ideas about life. I hoped for his acceptance and prayed that we could help each other. Admittedly over the years I have learned that I must give unconditional love, but just as strong over the years did I have to grow spiritually. You don't know how much I want to pay it forward – to love accurately.

One winter day in 1987 Eric and I took a long drive and went to a carnival. We boarded a ride much like a fancy merry-go-round. Initially the ride was predictable and fun. I kept sliding into Eric on the seat as centrifugal force squeezed me into him – so I tried to move back. Then the horror happened. The carnival ride attendant walked away from the ride as we were still on it. We both screamed – me out of fear and Eric out of anger. Neither of us knew if the ride attendant would return. The minutes seemed like hours. As I closed my eyes in fear Eric spied the attendant smoking a long cigarette. Finally it stopped abruptly when the attendant heard Eric's assertive voice. We were free at last. Eric's assertiveness had proven effective. As a lesson I have learned not to panic in certain situations and how to keep my composure when needed. Most importantly, I will not get on a ride at a deserted carnival in the wintertime. Let the truly adventuresome do it.

The next letter I show is to Eric in August of 2013.

Dear Eric:

I care about your well-being more than you know. Although I am not privy to your understanding of the world, I want to be supportive of your endeavors and actions. Please know that I love you and respect you as a man.

There have been times when you have called when I did not know what to say. To be honest the reason I have been like that is because I fear that I would influence you to actions which may not be to your benefit. I have wanted to encourage you to healthy choices and so I do not want to concentrate on the negative. Look, sincerely I want to give unconditional love and I do not wish to criticize like I used to. I want to change how I act. The real dilemma comes when I am giving unconditional love and then I see a real difficulty in one of your decisions. What do I do then? The risk is run for me to support you in something that may hurt you, or to be disliked for non-support.

Please let us have openness, acceptance and patience. Let us take the time to consider options and alternatives. All this, so we do not squash your energy or intentions. You have many talents and abilities and with work we all can be optimistic.

I thank you so much for your relationship and pray for your wellness. Let's talk some more when we can.

Only love,

Bob

My parents have always told me that they prayed for me and wanted me. They have always shown love and concern. I always felt at home with them until the rebellious preteens. It was then I personally tried to push against the dependence which was offered to me. My strivings for independence lasted into my twenties while my decisions were irresponsible. Sensitivity coupled with emotional immaturity lead me astray and brief, but acute psychosis disabled me. Could someone have given me amphetamines? Does withdrawal from phenothiazines cause psychosis? Certainly some anti-depressants cause psychosis in certain people – why not me? Have I and my family suffered the cruel hoax of me becoming a drug addict in my life? Why so many pills?

I both love my parents for their devotion to not only me but the entire family and for their willingness to try to love me despite my bad decisions. I feel guilt for taking the attention away from my sister and her family. That is why so much I have written about my original family wishing that circumstances would be different. When one member of the family demands so much attention it has been shown that other members feel a burden and are many times resentful.

I want less attention in my family and I hope to pay it forward to them. Sincerely I want to take some nice action for my direct family and for my sister and parents.

A letter to my original family dated March of 2006

Dear Mother and Dad: (Warminster Penna.)

Dear Annette: (San Diego, Calif.)

Something has really stood out in my relationship with you three members of my original family. That is one of my most glaring shortcomings. I need to know how to stop it – especially now.

It is fair to say that when I was eight years old, Annette was fourteen and you – the parents -- were adults. For me – it was like having three adults – three parents – who looked after me. In some ways I was cared for and in others I needed to grow up. I stayed young in heart and maturity. I really wanted to grow up as well and have the advantages of an older age. Even then I quickly learned that pacts and deals could be made with Annette my older sister. I could stay up later if I did not tell the adults if Annette's boyfriends came over when she watched me on weekends.

Furthermore, I could not hide the fact that I needed to give love, to one, to you, to all. I believed the world could be a better place for all if we worked for it – but could not understand that I had to put the focus on myself and take care of my own needs, because there is no good for the many if individuals do not take care of themselves. Carrying this lack of true discipline, lasted for me, well into adulthood, until I hit the drudges of my life in young adulthood -- making me either die, or become sane, clean and sober. I never even knew what to do first. Life was so confusing.

All at once I was troubled, irreverent, sloppy, compulsive, "fun" loving, a "goof off", the youngest of a family, a practical joker, worried, upset, irrational, a social animal, selfish, moody, sullen, argumentative, sad, angry, obsessed, fearful, aggressive, insane, out of reality, and even a little paranoid. How was I to get back? How was I to find a home?

The "old view" from the "therapeutics" was to say that it was my mother's fault. So I "bit their hook" and began to put pressure on Mother. She caught the brunt of it and the worst of me.

Nothing could have made matters worse and nothing could have been further from the truth. There was now too much aggravation, animosity, and aggression. Pain has lasted through life totally due to my attitude. I did not show true love. The true view from my heart is that when the heat was on me I beat those close to me with words. My actions did not help – they only made relationships worse.

In the end I made my Mother defensive, shy, and sensitive around me as my sister would call me confrontational.

What is Reality for me?

The true reality for me is contingent on exaggeration and hyperbole.

Each of the original Franz's is assertive in our own right. Where others melt when pushed into a corner I learned early to ague and fuss.

When I felt criticism I have pulled out all stops and fought with angry words. It is at these times I have not showed understanding and love. It is at these times I need to care more.

Even now I search for powerless people so I can fight for their rights. I am ashamed to say that at times I have enjoyed being the heavy – the bully in protecting those who are weak and helpless. I am sorry my confrontations come out of unbridled assertiveness. I am ashamed to say that I have used words as knives instead of charisma.

For that I ask you my family – please help me be the man I want to be. I admire the gentle – why does the Bull or Stallion show up?

It is important to convince using words not formed as weapons.

Please … let me use patience instead of overdoing everything. Please, let me show the strength you have given me.

Please pray.

A lot of love,   Bob

Now in 2013 my sister is seeing to it that our parents are getting the best care they can receive by finding a secure home to live in near her hometown. They have the luxury of being at least ninety years old, taken care of, and able to reflect on their lives. They are near Annette's adult children and great-grandchildren. Only few in the world can find this happiness. We are fortunate.

Annette was firmly rooted with her family – not like me who "followed" my parents as Dad lead across the country despite my sickness. Annette built "nests" while I attempted to run after the original family. It is necessary to slow down and do everything step by step.

Now I need to change. For me to find this change I have to use religion and education. Religion came in a spiritual community and education came by cultivating the mind so that discipline could be used. These processes make me appreciate procedures and bring me back to the very basics. Not only must I inhale for strength – but I must take two steps backwards to find where I am and carefully step forward. The labor comes when Bob does everything backwards first. First I have to see where I am.

This technique is not really a technique but a method. It is a way to solve life's problems as they come up. The pause backwards before the journey is taken is recommended to

114

others. Not only can we soak in the environment – but one determines his actions or mindsets as well. To be prepared means that one is ready for action.

Bob does everything backwards.

Leslie Jeanne and I have history because we have offered each other our hands for over twenty-five years. There are times we talk animated and there are times we are quiet and just "be." Sometimes we are separated during the day and sometimes we can be "joined at the hip." But above all, right as we speak – we are truly best friends. I do not believe that either of us can see otherwise. Here shown is a letter written to her in April of 2007.

Dear Teribear Love:

As you know, Teribear, this gnarled old anima is playful at times. I'm also a hopeless romantic. We have worked for this joy we share and to keep it going we have to keep our borough private. Don't you agree?

Look, I'm sorry about some of our past and I don't want it to affect our future. There was a time we needed a shaman. One who could interpret dreams and cast spells. Instead we got two psychiatrists, a counselor, and a case manger. You handled this pretty well and I could tell the pain wasn't directed at me. Your headstrong rebelliousness turned into fear of being hospitalized and you did not take the next step of self-destructiveness. You did not get hospitalized while your pain was watching and facing life's changes.

I love Teribear for her shy and timid ways. I love my Leslie Jeanne for her strength of spirit and her faith. I feel her love for me is strength. Beauty is simple and love is in the spiritual world. I promise you that if there is any way I can come back to you after the earthly death, I will. I ask you, though, to not come looking for me. Spirits may be encumbered at times; soothsayers may be too crafty in an earthly sort of way.

Please remember to dream. Whereas night dreams can show more about inner forces, desires and motives; wakeful dreams, or daydreams, can show more about possible behavior, wakeful mental constructs and mindsets. Also, what we choose to tell the other is of utmost importance to what we want the person to see in us. Getting to know you through your dreams has been as important as cooking breakfast. I love you, Leslie Jeanne.

I prefer to think that to be ready for a connection from God, one should prepare as best as possible. This means to hone out death, and to bring purpose, and balance to the senses. I believe to know that there is some entity – which I call God – that put us here and let us evolve. Einstein said, "The world is too ordered for it to be otherwise." To me, he believed in God. The Native Americans who worshipped a "Great Spirit" and all the psalmists of the Old Testament believed in God. For me deep inside these hurting physical beings are other spirits which yearn to be with the Almighty, "Higher Spirit." Someday we'll weave like strands of string and yarn in a beautiful macramé. We even do some of this now.

It doesn't matter what other people say, I am a mentally ill person who needs God. I believe that most people would do better with a God to care for – or a God that cares for them. Now I have made a decision; I need Christ and his teachings, and a mode of expression. I am not perfect, this church may not be perfect, yet it is the best we can do under the circumstances. There is a space in my head that can be filled with God and I accept this. With this in mind no pain, no doubt, will stir such troubles again. "Though I am a Christian – I am the least of all."

I love you so much, Teribear, - join me now, towards distant horizons.

A lot of love to you,

Mr. Teddiest Bear.

My family has marriages that have lasted long term. One of the keys to the phenomena is that the members accept what comes in life. Another key comes when there is respect for each partner's view. But above all, in my view it is the ability to become inspired by the simple image of your partner.

I have to see my partner in many ways as she is also inspired. Gatsby loved Daisy in F. Scott Fitzgerald's <u>The Great Gatsby.</u> In Shakespeare's <u>King Henry IV (parts 1&2)</u> the military's Hotspur genuinely loves his wife. I have heard and listened to songs in <u>Fiddler On the Roof,</u> and finally, I've studied and prayed over the station of Veronica as she wiped the face of Jesus in the Catholic's <u>Stations of the Cross.</u> We need to look for and find these inspirational examples of the caring between men and women. Gays and lesbians may welcome this as well – Aw hell, let's include everyone – all LGBT communities.

Remember, people do love each other. If you do not feel this -- then please go find someone and offer them a good deed.

EIGHTEEN

A MESSAGE

When I was a senior in high school our psychology class took a field trip to Napa Sonoma State Hospital. This trip scared the hell out of me because of my identification with the helplessness of the patients. Not only was it the first time I had seen the inside of a mental hospital, but it was the first time I felt like something could be wrong with me. I shook and perspired profusely.

I remember talking to a young male patient who said he didn't know where he was going when he left the hospital. In fact, his doctor would not let him leave until he had a place to go. I wondered how he would find a place to live as long as he was "stuck" in the hospital. The dingy walls were a backdrop for his tears. He had no home and no one in which to turn. I, as a high school student, tried to help in conversation, but kept running into stops. It is frustrating to try and offer suggestions when I, myself, did not even know where I was going with the conversation. After exhausting all possibilities with this man I said, "I'm sorry, I cannot help you with you living arrangement."

To which he replied, "I knew you couldn't help me anyways – that's why I am here. I just wish to two of us could just change places."

When I tried to put myself in his shoes I felt this feeling of utter helplessness mixed with fear. Something had to be done – but what?

I firmly believe that mental patients need more choices. *There needs to be more active participation by patients in the decisions of their lives.* A patient being totally helpless is another cause of stigma because of the perception in society that those who are vulnerable have to be weak in their dependence. Quite to the contrary – when patients band together and call themselves "mental health consumers" they appear much stronger as if choice was put back in their lives.

What I didn't realize when I was admitted to Delaware State Hospital was that I was lucky enough to have a place to go once I left the hospital. I had the luxury of calling the staff "bullies and female dogs" because I didn't have to rely on them in the long run. Even though the staff adopted the role of caretaker or "benevolent dictator" I do not have to accept their authority other than when I am there. The rest of the time I feel I do not have to ask for mercy.

All of the staff, including psychiatrists, had become caretakers. If they really want to be catalysts to health instead of mere caretakers or "babysitters," then they have to teach a discipline to freedom. I have gone from patient to client and then to mental health consumer. For my brothers and sisters, I can say, "We can God Bless the psychiatrists for being protectors, but our ultimate cost is stigma towards a vulnerable position." This truth means that the public believes that mental health consumers have sanity only as controlled by psychiatrists and the medical profession. Sadly, I say it is not true in most cases.

In any and every way possible we must be responsible for ourselves. Help another, quit smoking and cleaning the common room area are only little ways responsibility can be shown. Pay your bills and debts, "fess" up to that deed, and no cop outs, are bigger responsibilities. There needs to be more dignity of choice in patient's lives. We must find rewards not from "pats on the back" but from our own decisions making capabilities. Take charge of your own life. Do not be influenced by others especially if they want to shield you. Free will is our destiny.

I am a miracle because of my recovery. It is worth it even though sometimes it is slow and difficult, and just as this book was written over time, so my recovery grows over time. It is a developmental spiritual awaking, one in which I keep moving. I am not the same as when I began whether you read these writings or not. All of us change through time and the journey has been worthwhile.

Therefore, how may I find contentment?

I will find contentment by fitting into society in a satisfying niche, by having a healthy attitude with family and friends, and by having decent work. This includes prevention of admission into hospitals and institutions, and includes thinking with no psychosis, appropriate use of emotions, and remaining spiritual. Cherishing love in life will overcome hardships, also.

Now, my Teddy Bear is safe within my arms. I am going to keep him at home, so that he does not get lost again and learn from his experience. Who could be a better teacher? My Teddy Bear is soft, cuddlesome and furry. We feel grateful to have him back home. Grab yours and bring them on the next journey. Thank you and God Bless. It is 1998.

Terribear says, "Our time is up and it's time to close – Ted E. Bear, "O…Ted E. Bear why are you growling so?"

"You didn't think that a teddybear could growl like this, huh. Teribear?" says Ted E Bear.

Teribear says, "Not you, Ted E Bear, by all means. Why growl?"

"I growl knowing that my 'teddy doctor' has plans for me," retorts Ted E. Bear.

"I did not know that us 'teddies' *had* doctors," replies Teribear.

"It's true," states Ted E. Bear quite soberly, "And for now I am obliged to my 'teddy doctor'."

Innocently Teribear asks, "What does your doctor want you to do?"

"The doctor wants me to change medicine," Ted E. Bear growls.

But Teribear says this, "Oh, I see how that can be disturbing. You think it's easy for the doctor to say and hard for you to do."

"From witnessing how other doctors have done this in the past I certainly haven't been enamored to the process. Who knows what will happen?" says Ted E. Bear.

"Remember," states Teribear, "you are always part of the process."

"It's just another one of those things that may be too much," laments Ted E. Bear.

"So you are afraid of losing something close?" gently probes Teribear.

Ted E Bear hunches his shoulder, "Sniff...Sniff... I shouldn't be too sad, Teribear, the doctor is trying to help, but I am just not at my best yet, and you my dear, I don't want to lose my Teribear."

Teribear puts her paws on his face and says, "Oh, you'll never lose me Ted E. Bear. I know that I'm just stuffed cloth with buttons, but you'll never lose me. I love you."

"I love you." I said knowing that my body will also turn to dust someday and spirits will raise us.

Most of this writing was completed before 2000. Now I write in March of 2009. There is no doubt that I was raised by kind parents, and I cannot understand why I have not had the relationship with them that I desired. I almost feel that I was possessed by an entity which does not allow me to be honest when talking about my original family. For the most part I have been ashamed of my reaction to them, yet I really yearned to love.

Yes, there have been times when maudlin and histrionic airs had been taken when talking with teddy bears or about Mother, Dad or sister. I had used these descriptions and ended up making them seem simple or "trivolized" as Annette, my sister would say. In other words – what I said did not come out as accurately as I wanted to describe. My sister, my mother and father were not portrayed accurately.

I have trouble communicating the way I want and need to. Yet, I have the energy to try – at least to make the attempt. Most of my life I have tried to communicate and re-communicate until the truth finally resolves to come. That is why I do not mind you seeing the past attempts – which are in these writings – as well as more recent attempts – like right now. Most of these passages are over a decade old, but I have changed as have we all. Now my family may tolerate more differences of opinion. We are healing in a little better way. There have been many changes in ten years. What you have seen in these passages are snapshots of an evolving process of a sick man getting well.

Now, my parents – for whom we are blessed with at this writing – are doing as best they can in a retirement center in Pennsylvania – an hour by car from Northern Delaware where Leslie Jeanne and I live. Gracefully we all age and emotionally we care for each other. We pray for each other. My sister, Annette lives with her family in San Diego. We are all closer because of friendliness over the miles.

The older passages in this writing reflect my social illness at the time. What I am trying to say is that I am evolving to be a better man. True, I have sounded immature and not really honest. Yet, with practice honesty comes just like peeling layers off an onion.

I have needed my family more than they have needed me. I don't blame them if they get angry with me, but each relationship has been a godsend. It is good practice and loving business when one can help family and friends. In any climate I want to care and love people. Through the years they did not see what I saw just as I could not see from their vantage point. Our perceptions were different and only when that stark fact is accepted then we can begin to trust each other. This takes time and time is a precious community to lose.

If I am responsible for other people's perception, does that make my perception wrong? We all look at the mountain from different vantage points. What is yours?

One of my favorite lines is this:

"At times I may not like everyone – but I love each in their own special way."

God Bless you. I just want peace for all of us. It would be nice if we all could actively care for others.

Please Lord; Help us serve each other so that all of us may find a spirit of caring lovingness.

NINETEEN

THE WEDDING

Teribear Leslie mused with pride, "Ted E. Bear – Do you remember our wedding day?"

"How could I forget Teribear?" said Ted E. Bear. "Our wedding day was so very nice even despite my attitude at the time. I still apologize for the frame of mind which I carried."

"Mr. Ted E. Bear – no one knows what you are thinking unless you tell them. Yes, I thought that our ceremonies *were* wonderful."

"That much was right – but for me all the events and people seemed difficult to take."

Leslie Jeanne Breton and Robert N. Franz III were married on Sunday 8/28/88 at Saint Mary Magdalen Parish in Wilmington Delaware. Forty-four guests attended the service and reception including those from Shreveport Louisiana, San Jose California, Minneapolis Minnesota, Beech Grove Indiana, Pittsburgh Pennsylvania, McLean Virginia, as well as a local following.

At the time – I, ('Bob') was working at the Kirkwood Detox as a counselor. Since both Leslie and I saw no value in alcohol and drugs we jointly decided not to serve alcohol at our reception. Only a "dignified" celebration would be welcomed. Judge now if you feel that the ceremonies were "normal" for a wedding.

Initially – Leslie and I could not marry in the Catholic Church until we went to four lectures by older married couples as well as complete a computerized survey which determined how we would get along as a married couple. The lectures were long and boring mostly about the rhythm method of birth control and the results of the survey told us that we would have to work diligently at getting along with each other. To some extent we knew we would have to work at communication – something we have worked at for the past 27 years. Despite the church's difficult opinion of our relationship we were determined to have our way and marry anyways.

Second, our "dignified" wedding had gotten off to an auspices start. We could not obtain a wedding license from the State of Delaware until I brought a letter of permission to the Recorder of Deeds from my psychiatrist. So because I had once been committed to the state hospital I could not marry until I brought a note from my doctor. Stupid or not – she proudly acquiesced – and I brought her note. Both the State of Delaware and the Roman Catholic Church had profoundly affected our relationship.

A glitch occurred that I was not aware of at the time. The church organist did not show up. Luckily, one of the bride's guests, Michael Davidson, was an even more accomplished organist who stepped in and played beautiful music – "Pachelbel Canon" never sounded so good to Leslie's ears. [Michael was more than an archangel to my newly welcomed bride.] Although the music soothed me, I was more nervous about what was to come.

An 89 year old Catholic Priest of the Oblates of St. Francis de Sales named, Reverend John Conmy, [pronounced "Father CON Me!!"] officiated at our wedding. During his lifetime I found out that he had been a strict novice master in his order which showed in his traditions and conservative ways. He had a following of housewives and retirees who would gather one day each month to pray the rosary and listen to his views. My Mother was one of those women – that is how he came to us for the marriage ceremony.

The day before our wedding Father Conmy had returned from an extended visit to Rome and he was unusually tired. He looked pale – even paler than he already was – and also looked as though he could topple over at any second. At one point he paused and almost fainted on the altar. His exhaustion during the Mass necessitated us to remind him in whispers that we had to exchange our rings to which he became a little 'miffed'. A few moments later he told me again on the altar that since I was the Catholic member of this marriage it was necessary for me to swallow a "slosh" of the white wine. Full of aplomb – I sheepishly drank from the cup. A bittersweet taste came to me from more than my mouth. I felt warm – too warm. I was now uncomfortable at my own wedding. It was too late to apply for a "Papal Blessing".

As I have written, I was employed as an alcohol counselor at the Kirkwood Detox. It was not a place where I would find friends. Yet many chronic alcoholics liked me because I handed them unfiltered cigarettes. Not having friends I had to scrounge to find people to be in my wedding party. I found two sober guys who took pity on me and agreed to wear tuxedoes and be groomsmen. But it was not scrounging when I asked the man I loved more than any other man in my life to be my best man. Dad --- after some hesitation – did agree. Although it may have been awkward, luck had brought it that I could fill all three of the groom's positions. "Onwards to Marriage"—I then mused as we all got ready.

One question I have not answered here is what does 'marriage' mean in my family? [To us, marriage means to continue communication in a sustainable relationship with committed good will with a long term partner. It is an intention for a valuable, interpersonal, long term joining – or friendship. Speaking for my sister Annette I must say that she raised three children in a solid marriage. In my case, I try to streamline my life and have good will to all the people affected – children as well.] My sister and I now witness our parents after having well over a half century of marriage and while they are both nonagenarians, they lie down in a bed to take naps at the same time holding hands. They still care for each other. We live longer when we "team up".

A very important person we had to consider was Eric – Leslie's teen age son. Truly I wanted him to be welcomed and be part of something substantial. It was arranged for him to dress in a tuxedo – sit near the altar – and hold both rings. This "worked" believe it or not. [I have always been a dreamer.]

Just the day before the wedding Eric and I were driving across town and at the mention of our newly melded family I had to stop and actually vomit out of nervousness. Through his gales of laughter I accepted this as a sign that he would accept me as his Step Dad. I have always tried to believe that this "melded" family could help all of us. There are other times I question life; yet I always see the big wheels keep rolling onwards. I do not understand Eric's stubborn strength; neither do I want to believe that I cause resentments.

It ended up for me, to be like one who has stopped weaving in and out of traffic and by finally driving in the car line, have peace come gently sit next to me. I don't know what it is like for other people, but by reaching out in awkward ways I've probably caused more damage. Reading **_Soul On Ice_** or **_Black Like Me_** may help in understanding, but if as far as one goes is just to wear San Francisco sporting team hats, or to have license plates on your car that say "Motown", or to be 'Kool' in language, then much does not change as far as the race issue is concerned. Eric has an Afro-American background and I want to help him. Who says that is possible?

"Nothing changes if nothing changes." If people refuse to talk, or even fail to find common ground to agree on, then the free fall is treacherous. At least in this family this has shown to be true. Members of the family deny what they look like. Here, sometimes I am just not welcome or privy to all conversations. In my view just because I have two strong arms doesn't mean that I can help. Nothing for me is how the world was painted to my view in my youth. Still, though, I keep my commitments and values.

At the DuPont Country Club during the reception my bride and I fed cake to each other gently. Virtually all of the wedding party had their picture taken while in the country club even though many snuck out for cigarettes. Guests tried to loosen up because of no mood changing drugs being present at the reception. Dorothy stole my left shoe and as guests passed it around out of my reach I became increasingly frustrated. Our entire lives were changing to the tunes of "Pachelbel Canon" and "Happy -- To Be Stuck with You". Time, at the reception seemed to go on for an eternity. I wished so much to be alone with my new bride. I had never desired to be alone with her as I did right before leaving our wedding reception.

The first night after the wedding we stayed at a hotel in the city of Baltimore's Inner Harbor. That night the remnants of a passing hurricane leveled gales of rain on the hotel. Twisting winds had lifted the cloth awnings on the hotel crashing them on to the street. When morning came sunshine peeked through the clouds and the weather lifted.

That night, though, we were at peace because we were safe – Who knew what was to come? It was official – the journey had begun.

Second

PREFACE

For most people, it will be necessary to read this preface before reading any of the chapters to see how this book was written, and to see a thread between the chapters. This will put the chapters in perspective and bring continuity to the manuscript.

Please picture stepping up a spiral staircase and looking out away from the center of it. My view of reality is from the center as I ascend higher yet I am never really on it or even look towards it. Reality therefore can never be seen; instead I rely on each subject step to hold me up. As a result I skirt around reality relying on each step to connect to it as I concentrate on the next step up. This is how I see this book and this is the image I am using now.

My anima, my Teddy Bear, has been placed high atop a pine tree by some human or by some small animal. It is way out of reach and I need it to go on. For this reason I have to traverse the inside of the pine tree to the very top and reach to get my Teddy Bear. Climbing these branches is a step up onto a spiral staircase and holding the Teddy Bear again is like returning to sanity. The branches are as these chapters, some I see directly, and others shoot out in different concentric directions. Some are sturdy and some are not. At all costs I must get my Teddy Bear back unless I hurt myself or somebody else. When I have Teddy Bear, I feel comforted and in control of my life.

Read this book as if every chapter is a branch emanating from the reality of my life. There could be more branches or there could be less, but to climb to Teddy Bear each must be used for a firm foothold. Furthermore, please realize that something could be described as a well thought out feeling yet not be totally accurate to another person. That is to say that something that motivates me to action may not motivate someone else. Second opinions are welcome but not always used.

The medical profession, family, friends, schools, and even the clergy can help guide me close to the pine tree truck of reality. For me, certain medications are necessary as well.

You may as, "Why all of this fuss about a 'teddy' in a tree?"

I say, "If the problem of sanity could be solved with one person, just think of how it could be generalized to help the many. Come Home Teddy Bear! Please, come home."

Each chapter branches of from the true reality even though they begin at a real trunk.

SECOND

INTRODUCTION

My purpose is to write a manuscript which can be shown to medical professionals, especially those who will prescribe medicine for my use. I do not want irresponsible people to give me medicines or treatment that cause adverse reactions. I feel doctors in my past have caused such misfortune.

To make my point, I have to give some sort of history to the doctors. All of this writing grows into a full blown manuscript with not only psychiatric history, but with moral and ethical questions considered as well. I deal with my mental illness and try not to be ashamed. I describe what this illness does to my family and how I fit into society.

The manuscript is "eclectic" in the sense that it draws from all aspects of my life showing just how pervasive mental illness is. It is as if a "virus" has permeated me – physically, mentally, and spiritually. It causes me to have all my efforts focus on the eradication of this "virus". There are signs, which I am aware of now, that lead down the path to insanity. As long as I have these signs I know what to work on for sanity.

Mental illness, as far as I know, is not caused by a virus. It is not a demonic possession nor is it due to lack of intelligence. My firm belief is that it is a genetic predisposition which can be triggered by events, or stages in life. My pain throughout life has been isolation, although as I grew older I learned how to balance each situation as it comes up. The older I get, the better I get (so far). For me, medicine is not everything and I must be responsible for my own behavior. However I would be foolish to say that medicine did not play a role.

Whatever happens, difficulties can be worked through if all parties can deal decently with each other. I refer specifically to doctors who take people off some medicines so abruptly that dangerous consequences are a result. Even though in actuality, the doctor may be trying to stop a condition termed *tardive dyskinesia* – which is disabling-the methods are still crude and archaic. There must be more research and there must be more explanation and mercy.

There are and will be many more medicines in the coming years. At this point in time I have taken upwards of twenty five psychotropic medicines in a period twenty four years and see no need to take more. Some bring me to depression and others set me off into mania. No longer can I live at the whims of doctors. Their impetuosities about prescribing so quickly make it rough on me. Life has got to be different, because throughout these years it has been very confusing, to say the least.

After much turmoil in my life, I turn to God but haven't surrendered all of my strength yet. I turn to God because it is through positive signs, which I will recognize, that will lead me the rest of my days. I pray this manuscript will help some people – it helps me to write.

WHY ME!? STOP IT!

ONE

LOVE

Love is the healer now in 1994. My struggle is to be positive physically, mentally, emotionally, and spiritually. When I take refuge in the positive I am even tempered, motivated, productive, and in fellowship with others. I seek no enemies and take no hostages. We are ready for a future.

"I love you," I said rolling over backwards amidst the pillows. We were snug on top a flowered comforter in our dark bedroom.

"I love you, too, Ted E. Bear," Leslie Jeanne said.

"Is my teddybear through worrying now? Oh, my Ted E. Bear just worries so much!"

"I'm not worrying anymore," I said.

We lie there quiet for a moment, I on my back and Leslie Jeanne gently tossing one leg over my left leg. Hugging, we were face to face as we talked.

"I am so glad you are not worrying now. But it didn't feel like you were worrying *that* much. I mean it didn't get in the way of our love," Leslie Jeanne said.

I responded, "I may not have felt that way – but I can always conjure something up. Would you like to hear what I'm thinking now?"

"Sure," she said languidly.

"Why do you call me Ted E. Bear?" I queried.

"Because you are so fuzzy and cuddly and you've always been good to me." She whispered in my ear.

"And Teribear, I've always loved you more than you know." We embraced once more as my mind went over exactly why I call her Teribear." It is short for "Mother Theresa of the Teddy Bears." As a nurses aid in a geriatric center her gentle ways are greatly needed. She is my 'teddybear' – my "Teribear" always.

We embraced once more and fell off – as one, our lives become luscious sultry warmth once again.

Leslie Jeanne and I are different in many ways yet we make a solid couple. This month we are married ten years and have reason to celebrate. Our psychological histories are vastly different and it seems strange that our relationship matches up so well. So far we have disproved all guessers.

In one way our background is similar. My father, as her father, had worked for a multinational chemical corporation. Both families had moved around parts of the United States finally to settle in Wilmington, Delaware. Each of the parents in that generation had to deal with the difficulties of the Great Depression and did not understand a new generation with high disposable income. On the other hand Leslie Jeanne and I were weaned onto the recordings of the Beatles and each of us could drive an automobile by the time we were sixteen.

My religious background is Catholic and Leslie Jeanne's is Christian Science. Although the religions are mutually exclusive, there are good points to both. In my experience Catholics tend to be more pragmatic in worship with complex doctrine. But, the people in the Christian Science faith, to me, seem to "expand their minds" more as they transcend to the simple life. Ceremonies seem to be more important to Catholics while reading is more important to Christian Scientists. Many of those faithful actually use "Christian Science Reading Rooms" more than they would their church buildings. To them: 'Spirit is real; matter is unreal'.

All of this is very interesting to me but I can only go a little ways further because at this point in time I do not know much about religion. Suffice it to say that now Leslie Jeanne is baptized Catholic and we both became regular church goers. She needs the ceremony and I need information. We are motivated by our inspiration and our love for each other.

Leslie Jeanne is my partner (wife) whom I go through life with. She is kind even when thinking of herself. She is gentle and has compassion. She is a mother to one and a fool to no other. She cares not to be a burden to others, yet aids others by putting them into her routines. Leslie Jeanne has hygiene routines. She is "Obsessive-Compulsive." Although this writing does not go into depth about OCD – it does talk about mental illness. Because of my love for her and because of my uxorious nature I will protect her if anyone gives her trouble. She knows this.

Illness in general and OCD in particular does not sit well with Christian Science because medicine is needed. Painful as all of this is, Leslie Jeanne adjusts by bonding with me to find a better way to deal with our respective diseases.

I have the diagnosis of *schizoaffective bipolar type* – given to me by some professionals. What this really means is that my moods are out of touch with my environment in a high-low cyclical fashion. I also must take medicine for this condition – medicine that is much different than Leslie Jeanne's. Perhaps the greatest thing about our relationship is that at anytime we can get out of ourselves and concentrate on the partner. She respects and observes my moods and erratic sleep patterns. I can spot repetitive action and total focus on one subject. Whereas I fit into a time schedule, she fits into intimate conversation. As it turns out we each can appreciate routines and we each love long intimate endeavors.

We do best as a couple when we have one and one half hour a day where we can spend time together. The relationship needs a high amount of time together but is not necessarily high maintenance.

Unlike those in my family, who once a disease is pointed out will take the prescribed treatment, I have noticed that people in Leslie Jeanne's original family will not admit to illness. Or if they do, then no treatment will be used at all unless it is from a designated "healer." This tendency remains true today even though Leslie Jeanne's parents do not consider themselves current practitioners of all the Christian Science beliefs. They may use the older traditions if in a pinch – but even now her parents each find that their beliefs have morphed to a degree.

Leslie Jeanne uses my family as support and hides all disease – even a sore tooth – from her mother and father. This is one time when philosophy is overshadowed by guilt and emotions. In my view traditions and behaviors change through time only if we are allowed to be comfortable. Medicine draws from science as religion makes claims as well.

"I'm OK. I don't want you to ask me if I'm OK because I'm Okay! Everything is just fine," whispered Leslie Jeanne.

"I know. You give off signals too." I responded.

Again we lay side by side touching. A pause ensued.

"We are so successful because of shared agoraphobia. Don't you think it's true?" said I. Defining she said, "You mean fear of the market place?"

"Yes," I said, trying to act certainly, "My inclination is to compensate. If I feel self-conscious in the shopping mall I'll walk brisker and with more bounce in my step. Your solution is even better. You copy someone you see and walk slowly with a cup of coffee in your hand. Soon I am imitating your walk with a soda in my hand. After a conversation all the fear is gone."

"In the end it didn't feel like everyone was looking at me." Leslie Jeanne said proudly.

"Same here," said I.

"Bob," Leslie Jeanne was getting serious with me now. "Basically I don't want to analyze, but I feel our love works because of three things. First, we listen to one another. Second, we try to remain flexible and patient. Third, we do not become anxious or angry at the same time. Don't you think we do our best to put these principles into action?"

"You're probably right if you talk about in those terms," I said. "But what if we look at it in other terms? Such as, out of in-laws, money, and children, which could pull us apart?"

"Quit being that way. I don't like the way you say that," continued Leslie Jeanne. "We won't be pulled apart if we work together."

131

"I'm sorry I said that to you. You're right; we have to keep communication open about these topics. I do love you a lot Teribear. I mean every word I say."

"Right now," Leslie Jeanne stated, "The only communication I want from you is to say why you were worrying so much a little while ago. Won't you tell me?"

So I began with my fear. "There are times I see the raw ugliness of life. Five years ago I stood in a courtyard of the state hospital as a patient seeing only freezing rain, mud and cigarettes. People near me, the moon, and stars were invisible. My attitude was bleak and barren. No one could help me. I feel I could end up there again, but now there are buffers. I am taking medicine that works for me and I remain sober. There is a 'care' system of which I am part. There are loved ones whom I cherish."

"Yes," Leslie Jeanne interrupted, "we do have loved ones, so why worry? Doesn't worry show fear? Doesn't fear cause people to go insane? That's the crux of it. Your bitterness about your three years in mental hospitals is past tense fear. It'll drive you to the brink. Bob, I love you. We are here now."

"Forgive me for my bitterness," I replied, "I have lost all dignity in a slide downwards and only through much effort can I begin to climb the ladder out of this morass. Some would say that I was sick. Others would say the devil tempted me as a young man. I don't know which was right but it is a hard climb out and I do not wish it on anyone."

"I was going to say that I was on the same boat but now I hear you are in a morass. What next?" Leslie Jeanne asked.

"My solution from this screaming hell is spiritual in nature. I am forced by choice to become a substance abuser, then a recovering alcoholic, and then take the baby steps to becoming an infantile spiritual being seeking humility. I have had to compromise with the church of my youth, until finally it is possible to accept the unbelievable in *that* doctrine of *that* church. But nevertheless it is working and I can find some dignity in the church."

"You hurt too much Bob, you keep talking like this and you may get hurt again. I want the best for you – I want the best for us, as well. What will happen – will happen. Trust in God. Prayer, yes we need more prayer. Remember, Love is the healer. It is coming to me again." Then, Leslie Jeanne said what she wanted to say, "Loving is the most important healing I will ever have."

"Thanks," I said, "Let me lie here for a little while. I just want to think – not worry – just think."

"I suppose you want me to get up and cook dinner?" she jokingly said.

"Yes, it's your turn. It's also my turn to clean up so don't make a mess." I responded.

"What *are* you going to T-H-I-N-K about? Are you going to think about our minds, bodies or souls?"

"Maybe how they interact. Oh, I don't know. Give me some peace, woman. Yes, I love you. I've got to think about the thesis for the book I'm writing. You understand?"

"Of course I understand, after all I have a part in the book also" said Leslie Jeanne.

"I love you. Just go to the kitchen and I'll work on this." I said.

Now to work on any part of the thesis I have to make a number of paragraphs and then reduce, reduce, and reduce until I get the fewest words possible to describe exactly what I mean for the rest of the book. Leslie Jeanne reminded me that for most individuals who are mentally ill; fear is the major motivator in behavior. Fear, therefore, debilitates the mentally ill person. The rest of the thesis is already complete.

I talk to myself as I have thoughts on fear:

"Both disease and stigma create fear in an individual. I believe that each organism knows danger by illness or by other people's rejection and adapts behavior in reaction to this danger. This reaction is known as fear. The behavior explained is either due to short-lived, acute or chronic fear. Even anger, which is an irrational response to or because of fear, is a cause of mental illness.

But what of the scientific answers which deal with such substances as serotonin, dopamine, epinephrine, norepinephrine and even adrenalin. Cannot the ebb and flow of brain chemicals truly define fear? Therefore the simple 'language' definition saying that mental illness means fear is obsolete in scientific terms. In scientific terms all emotion comes from chemicals and nerves acting on and in the brain and brain stem. Hypothetically each individual has 'medicines' or chemicals which may act in a positive way on the brain and brain stem."

How do I say this in two sentences?

"Fear is a behavioral reaction, sometimes expressed as a mental illness, which is caused by chemicals acting on nerves. In healthy organisms, this emotion is integrated to a safe equilibrium."

What does that mean?

"Sometimes a person needs medicine to control emotion."

"That sounds interesting." Leslie Jeanne said as she came back into the room.

"Did you finish the thesis yet? I know you had some of it done already," she said surely.

"I'm still thinking about it," I said.

"Dinner's ready," she called to me.

"Good, because I'm hungry," and with an afterthought, "Besides I was talking to myself".

"Yes, I heard you, and you said you are not one of the mentally chosen. Both you and me and half the people we know are all crazy."

"Let's just say that maybe we should say an extra grace before dinner." I observed.

Left on the bureau in the bedroom was a piece of paper with the following three paragraphs scrawled on it:

Thesis:

Currently society, professionals, and families, based on observations, decide who is mentally ill and what treatment is necessary for this mental health population. Furthermore, attitudes of self proclaimed, responsible parties create stigma for the mentally ill this preventing wellness.

A healthier approach is to have the client address the cause and definition of mental illness allowing for their own self determined measurable goals to define treatment. Treatment could be medicine therapy or psychoanalytic, but it must work cognitively and on emotions. Not until an active role is taken can the client reach his full potential.

Goals of the client may or may not be mutually agreeable with society, professionals, and families. For the client who is able to respond, intervening factors, such as religion and education will play a large part in the improvement of health.

TWO

GIFTS

"Dear God, Bless this food Lord, and bless us and tell us what to do with this book," I prayed.

We dined on baked chicken breasts smothered in barbeque sauce with canned corn, and a three bean salad out of a jar. Satiated and after my cleanup Leslie Jeanne sat me down.

"Look, you want to know how to write this book," She said, "Do you know what exactly you have to put in it?"

"I need a timetable put in it as early as possible." I replied.

"Then put it into the book – right now."

Bob's Timetable - (directly from his notes)

1952	Birth
1959	First Communion
1967	EAGLE Scout Award
1968	FIRST REAL DRUNK
1970	STUDY TRIP TO SIX EUROPEAN Countries
1971	High School Graduation / Enter College
1975	FIRST TWO Mental Hospitalizations
1976	Graduation from College
1978	TREATMENT with Orthomolecular Psychiatry
1980	FIVE Month Hospital STAY
1981	Consistent Attempts to stop drinking and using
1983	LAST DRINK
1986	Engagement with Leslie Jeanne
1988	MARRIAGE to Leslie Jeanne
1991	Beginnings of Journal
1993	LAST Psychosis / LAST Hospitalization
1998	Fifteen years of not drinking / Ten years of marriage.

(• The object here is to not drink or use, find no need for hospitalization, and to stay married.)

136

One of the problems with mental cases such as mine is providing continuity. Each event seems to be a flashback in which memories become jumbled. This not only affects my writing, but gives the reader a conflicting impression of events in my life. Although I do my best to put these events in their proper time, most essays have 'stories' in them which relate but are from different years. As a three year veteran of psychiatric wards all of the bullshit thrown at me in random order drives me insane.

Use the time graph if you have to know the chronology, otherwise read this material as a psychiatric person sees the events in his life."

Girls, homework, and play were my passions in my early years.

Dolly said, "Bob, I've found someone else – I don't think we can continue dating."

Molly said to me, "Bob, my Mom just feels uncomfortable around you. We really can't see each other anymore."

Polly said, "I don't believe this – you called to ask me how to make garlic bread? No! No! Don't call again."

Despite all this and more rejection, I did manage to have a girlfriend each year from kindergarten to senior year in high school. It was always necessary to have someone I could feel affection towards. Nicki, my kindergarten girlfriend walked hand in hand with me to the principal's office as we were admonished for playing "house" and hugging. Charlotte, who would be my fourth grade girlfriend, grabbed my attention by punching me in the stomach knocking the wind out of me right in the classroom. Each year there seemed to be a different style.

When I was young I dated female tennis buffs, thespians, secretarial students, and even one who wanted to become a psychiatrist. In spite of all of this interaction I really did not learn how to become friends with young ladies until years later. Proms and dances did not help me become close to women because there were so many of them and hormones ran too strong. Still I remained a hopeless romantic and felt grounded when I was close to a young woman.

While I was hopelessly in love when dating my grades suffered. Usually I was a pretty good student but when cupid struck I could not concentrate. Later in college I could not or would not let myself get close to women because I wanted to keep my grades up. I denied myself the pleasure of really getting to know anyone special. Fooling myself that it was a choice between academics and love; I became lonely. Males were friendly but I felt more competitive with them. Friends became objects to recreate with focus only on play.

With the sex drive I had it was not natural to deny myself a girlfriend because of grades. It was as though I had been hypnotized to cause such pressure in me. It wasn't just sex I needed – it was love. I wanted to reassure myself of love because denial of it brought me to despair and depression. There I was not ready for commitment but needing love.

So I was emotionally frustrated yet playing hard. If I couldn't get exercise playing pick-up-basketball or rugby, then I was drinking beer trying to find women or lost in the library studying diligently in a stupor. All of this was worse than I thought. I was better off getting sentimental at proms or venting emotions in high school plays. Somehow I learned that by drinking I saw the adolescent mood swings could disappear. Drinking became a dirty habit. By the end of college all I would do was study and drink with no avocations.

The obvious question arises; "What did my original family do to me to make me a drunk schizoaffective?" This question must be phrased differently. The more insightful but not so obvious question is – "How did my family give me enough strength to continue?" Still I am sensitive and will fight to defend my family.

Dear God:

I wish to stay calm about the changes in my life. I wish to be more flexible. I wish to react or not react to others but not to be so sensitive. I do not desire to be critical of others. I want to enjoy the fruits of this life.

Please let me have tolerance and patience. I want to be able to put one thing down when interrupted by another and pick it up again when others are complete. I want to be kind and make time for others when they need it.

In some way I want to make my life a service to people. I want to pay attention and listen to others. Make my deeds meaningful. I want to start small with words and deeds, take care of myself, and build on service to others while remembering love and forgiveness.

Sincerely,

Bob--1995

Because of my sensitivity to some drugs or medicine, and early hyperactivity and depression my relief only came with the proper medicine. I feel that I have a genetic predisposition for a mental disease. As a result my connections with others in relationships did not become satisfying until I was well into adulthood. Even at a young age when in high school and college I felt grandiosity and continual pre-paranoia. It felt like I was always the center of attention whether I was or not. Being the youngest and second born enabled me to have quite a lot done for me before having a trial at life for myself. Mom and Dad encouraged me to save my soul, care for others, and work hard, in that order. I will always remember those teachings.

From girlfriends to alcohol I should have read Menninger's 'Whatever Became of Sin?' in eighth grade instead of twelfth grade. I needed to find dignity in my life instead of being a victim of self centered fear.

Please Lord:

Give me the respect I desire, not for my ego and such,

But more for bringing help and a good human approach.

Let people trust me and have faith in me.

Let people treat me with dignity so that I may treat others right.

Let me live up to it, in faith and truth.

Bob--1996

I made turnarounds for the positive in school, and behavior which to this day I wonder how I ever had the strength. Most of these either were out of guilt or from the expectations of loved ones. Once I took Mom's car out for a drive, hit a fence, perfectly parked it in the garage, and spent the night in fear. When I was found out it became the last discipline problem for me in my young life.

At an earlier time this came about by receiving a poor math grade in 7th grade. There was so much shame that I worked hard and ended up in accelerated mathematics in high school. I was never diagnosed as mentally ill until age twenty. Now looking back, some verbal help may not have been so bad.

At my parents home the summer after my junior year in college I became totally psychotic for the first time. My parents had no idea what to think and took me to a drug and alcohol detoxification center where I was not accepted. Then they called a family doctor who later called a psychiatrist.

I don't have to tell you what I was thinking at the time. There was a mindset and a mental construct while my thoughts were scattered. I kept having one thought that religion was totally absurd and that it was causing tremendous sadness in my life. All my principles had left me. Since I wanted to be on a lunar plane, I dropped my pants and mooned the detox counselor and bent over for the doctor. Remembering all of this brings back fear for the laughter was too hard to take in my frame of mind. My life plans changed on that day. Any academic success I had was never translated into the life of this young adult.

My blindly naïve attitude which I reached as a senior in high school was soon becoming worldly in a sick sort of way. I wanted a break from my family simply because I was "of that age." Rebelliousness came with periodic psychosis and I resented the sage dominance of my original family members. I wanted a bride – feeling that another lover could take me from 'subservience' to freedom. Since I had been "sick" the relatives had to control me even closer. By age twenty-five I had the freedoms of a sixteen year old.

Life was enjoyable when young but it was my inability to come to grips with change that caused my stress. Furthermore, it was an all or nothing attitude that moved me to the breaking point. The pressure became too much as I honestly had no idea what to do when mental illness stuck. Does anyone?

Now, it is time to say what it is like for me to be schizoaffective yet healthy in this society.

Luckily I am married to a fine woman, unique in her loving ways. We have chosen and made the decision to live with each other indefinitely and care to help each other along the way. Others respect our marriage, as well, and dignify us with decency. I speak now of social agencies, family and members of church and self help groups. I (and might I say we) am (are) very grateful. This much remains true.

But living a life that is partially mainstream and partially "cared for" by agencies is not exactly satisfying to each of us individually. Waiting in line for medicine is no fun as counselors, nurses, and case managers watch and play favorites and on some days tell you where to go, and belittle you by talking about your "little words." Furthermore it is not fun to be coerced in staying at home only to wait for them to "check it out". All I need is the medicine – thank you.

Then again with the freedom I *do* have I am able to say or do almost anything. I *am* grateful for the medicine, but on that one day of the week when I am visited do they have to be so pervasive? It became this way when there were no more means to pay my medical bills. The State deemed it necessary that I live in this 1984 Orwellian scenario. For me it's easy – for real, it's all a matter of attitude. For others it can be more difficult. I'll continue trying to better myself, love those around me, and kill the rest with kindness (so to speak).

Living in the mainstream for me is like traveling through a subculture. I work in the yard of my parents, volunteer at the Alliance for Mentally Ill, and go to self help groups nightly. Other days I go to church meetings, and concentrate on poverty ministry, daily mass, or some other dogma. Until Eric, my stepson moved a distance; I would drive him around town. I work only when they let me. Also, sometimes I take long walks or exercise at the YMCA. See, I can do anything anyone else can do. Why am I a prisoner? I am a prisoner now because I cannot find work.

Just recently a manager of a pharmacy dangled a part-time minimum wage job in front of me only to take it away for the 'reason' that the main office had been hiring too many people. I may have smiled but I did not believe him. People talk in this town. Even if he were right about hiring too many people you can not exactly assume that people are not talking about others including you. Just ignore it. Comfort ability is relative. Glimpses of both sides are painful. Whereas the glint in the eyes of many is toward the almighty dollar; I am forced to live as a communist.

Actually it is how you look at it – I am a prisoner of my own mind, not of this country. I have needed time to heal from the shocks of the medical profession, cops, and social workers—the do-gooders who determine futures and really talk behind your back.

What can I do? I can go to the library and to the gym. I can quietly – without telling – look for work and perhaps get something. I can go to school until it comes out my ears or I can write. As long as a carrot appears this rabbit may be hopping to a place where there is a better life. Treatment has been harsh at times and I am not referring to fairness. It is true that my recovery has been slower than most. I refuse to jump up after every year and one half psychosis only to get a job and fail. Five years have passed since my last hospitalization and I continue to take my time. You can wait.

Let's look at the positives which will lead me to a better position. Relationships have always been important to me and these will be sustained. Everyday I affirm my love to Leslie Jeanne. Parents play a role from their well meaning expectations that I will stay well. Distant relatives will also play a role simply because they are present. Peers and self-help group members add camaraderie and goodwill, while finally church members smile and pray. All of these people tell me that we do have a place in this culture and society.

We need a place that is uniquely our own where we can give or take money, time, or love. My wish is for more security enabling me to have more freedom of will commensurate to my capabilities. It could be a matter of trust.

My wife is the object of all my earthly love with family a close second. I wish to serve the Lord most of all with the trust deserving of a deity. I cannot idly stand by while injustices are thrown to others, but unfortunately I cannot fight every indignity or action that causes strife simply because there are times I need to take care of myself. In this struggle for mental health rights there has to be a team effort.

Particularly disturbing to me is the issue of dominance. Virtually everyone in my life has some dominance over me. I tire of having to answer to them all because it's like taking the weight of an inverted pyramid on my mind, and soul. Push, prod, push, prod, supercilious carnivorous grins -- leave me alone. Instead of saying "My God will protect me," (which he will); so I'll just be more blunt as I say. "I am better than you – and, I believe this." Mark Twain said, "When you tell the truth you will never need a long memory." All of what is written is the truth.

In my second adulthood (which comes before second childhood) I will do as I wish. It will be a time of joy to be free to look certain others in the eye and "just say No," when they are trying to coerce me to do something. I'll respond, "Let's go to the gym and talk it over." Or I'll say, "Shall we go somewhere and pray over this?" Can they even consider such questions today in this "free" society? You may just end up saying, *"touché"* and follow your heart. Or maybe, just maybe, your heart may end up full of strength *and* joy.

Leslie Jeanne and I feel something from God that not many people feel. The joy we feel is but a by-product of this quality. No human, I believe, can reach to the limit as God does. The quality in question is – *unconditional love*. We feel this love from God and believe it will in some way continue. God Bless You.

THREE

THE ALCOHOL APPROACH

My Dad feels that my disease began when I was twenty – when psychotic behavior was first noticed in me. Actually I was having symptoms weeks, months and years before this age. I feel their was always mental illness inside of me and that it only manifested itself dramatically at certain times of great stress. Drinking alcohol was a way of alleviating uncomfortable symptoms and soon became a problem in its own right. Nevertheless, tremendous internal fear combined with confused mental logic made me helplessly psychotic a number of times in my early twenties. This was an illness that went to the core of my being – my genetics. Always sick; I was to recover.

Other people had other ideas about my illness:

"You are not like the other mentally ill – nor can you claim to speak for the mentally ill. Remember you are a manic depressive. To write about the mentally ill would be a misrepresentation," the phone counselor said to me.

"Ok, I'll do whatever you say," I said fully knowing that this lady did not know what she was talking about. From paranoid schizophrenic, to bipolar, this lady had never felt my gut, witnessed my many hospital stays, or never came up with the diagnosis of schizoaffective bipolar type that so many clinicians had found in me. I would never tell her. She would not learn from me of the many crossovers of symptoms in mental illness. I *will* write about the mentally ill from my own view especially for what I see, feel, and believe. I will do it from my own perspective and use myself as an example.

To do this I look at definitions of mental illness. There is the medical model of categories (DSM IV) with classifications of mental disease changing through time, even though populations remain with the same symptoms throughout the years. Second, there are genetic/biochemical definitions of illness in the brain which are aggravated when individuals interface with society. Third, there is the legal and societal view of mental illness which is a series of classifications ranging from the dull to the alarming. I'm sure there are more. My view is much simpler.

I believe that all mental illness is based on irrational fear and the reaction to this fear. From my definition there are many more mentally ill in this world than those who are just "certifiably" mentally ill. It is the reaction to fear which causes up to be anxious, insane, megalomaniacal, depressed or just plain mentally ill. To accept one's self is to accept the

143

condition of the brain; to not accept the individual condition means there is reaction "friction" and irrational fear.

I am mentally ill at times to the point of psychosis because of three reasons. Their can be interplay between these reasons but usually it only takes one to get me going. The first is the physical reality of what chemicals do to my brain. Illegal drugs and alcohol can and do send me out of reality. Some medicines which also "bathe the hypothalamus" can set me off. (Don't laugh – even a good workout can change brain chemistry). Brain biochemistry can affect the individual with a differential strength and a long lasting result.

Second, the mental emotions of a simple alcoholic (if indeed there is such a person as a "simple" alcoholic) cannot be regarded as disposable. So many times we hear the statement, "Well, he was just drunk," excusing the behavior but not addressing the emotions. If I react to these emotions then I must deal with guilt, shame, and false pride, lack of respect, dishonesty and denial. After a while, the cycle of emotions is rapid at a frequency when I am "high" and "low" alone on my own cranial juices. When a mentally ill individual drinks, everything eventually becomes exaggerated even after the drinking episode when one is so-called "sober". This "post acute withdrawal" causes overreactions and can last for months in the sick person. Mental functioning deteriorates in the mentally ill even with no outside chemical therefore the emotions become the exaggerated reality.

I have mentioned that brain chemistry and mental-emotional functioning determines mental illness. Now I add a personal-cultural component – the handling of myths. An example is shown here when I was age five. The next paragraphs I wrote in my journal in 1994:

"My fears have been irrational throughout my life. Besides the common baby fears of falling or abandonment I feared being stripped, fried and eaten at a very young age. I remember this irrational fear quite clearly and could not in faith blame Mother for instilling this fear in me. Somehow the fear had to do with the loss of innocence and chicken being prepared in the kitchen. I felt as though the chicken was being punished – with visions of hell – just as I was when sent to my room. It was my strict, sick, sense of religion and the formation of a conscience which made me believe that I would be cooked and eaten when doing something wrong. It was going to Catholic Mass where the priest made a fuss over the statement 'Eat my body---Drink my blood' which let me to imagine gruesome thoughts at the age of five.

At each growth stage thereafter I had fears which tormented me. Now they deal with people and society as old fears ferment when they don't fade away".

There are myths on a personal level and myths on a cultural level. How we handle these myths in life determines if we really are in reality. Look at Saint Nicholas and existence of heaven as anthropological versus religious concepts. Even in scientific circles there *was* a St. Nick, this has been documented, and his legacy carriers on. Whether on believes that his effect is more legacy than spirit or sprit than legacy depends upon your orientation. The existence of heaven also poses a problem. Nothing has been proven in the matter of life after death. Yet views from all sides claim to know infallible truths. Belief and faith give each individual their answer. Before judging another perhaps we should consider not just individual characteristics, but society and cultural as well. What one person sees as a fantasy or myth; another will see as reality. How we handle these differences determines our mental functioning.

Although the following encounter in 1968 was not my first with ethanol it did prove to be my first drunk.

Notice the image I have of John Wayne's persona in the following high school scene. Just as other myths, Hollywood's can mislead and misguide.

"So where are we going tonight?" I said to Jack and Ray, my two high school friends.

"We are going to Bert's," Ray said, "You know Bert – to spend the night and drink."

"Drink what?" I said nervously.

"Jack stole a bottle of 'Wild Turkey' from his Dad and it's in the trunk of my car," Ray said proudly.

Incredulously I said, "But, why do we have to drink with Bert? He's so … dorky."

"Look," Ray reasoned, "Bert is giving us a place to spend the night – we can all get drunk and have a place to crash. Don't you see?"

"That part is OK. So I guess I'll do it. Thanks." I said.

I cannot pinpoint when I became schizoaffective bipolar in my life but I knew when I made bad decisions. For me, drinking was a private affair even when done in public. Now I would have to show dominance since I was recently elected class president, and be gracious to the dorky – maybe even gay – Bert. I was not sure how the night would play out, but I was certain that if I drank like John Wayne did in the movies I could be a benevolent good-tough guy.

Later that school day Bert came up to me and uncharacteristically with bravado said to me, "Bob, we've got a hot night planned tonight. Are you sure you're up to it?"

"I'm up for anything you can do." I said unsure of all of the aggressive cockiness.

All he retorted was "Be at my house after the game."

So that evening after the football game I had Mom's car, a toothbrush and a sleeping bag over at Bert's Mom's place.

"Oh, so you're Bob Franz – I always wondered what a political class president looked like." His little sister sneered at me. Bert's Mother did not say a word as she glared at the TV. I was led to Bert's room while I wondered just what "Wild Turkey" would taste like. There would be no problem I mused, if I could just swallow it like John Wayne did in wartime movies. Jack and Ray showed up in Ray's car. Soon afterwards I pulled a short straw meaning that the four of us would leave for the evening with me driving my Mom's car. The other laughed, "Don't forget the booze. You know Bob wouldn't."

After driving to a secluded spot where we all smoked cigars, I said dizzily, "John Wayne never had it so good." A gale of laughter ensured. I felt that the other three were going to get me in trouble that night. Of course, any trouble I was to get into would be their fault and not mine. I felt they wanted to get me into a mess.

John Wayne came and went fast. In the sprawling growing suburbia I downed a good portion of the whiskey as it burned down my esophagus and into my stomach. I would always finish a gulp with an "Ahh" like the movie star's character. The last thing I remember is urinating in a foreign yard and being pinned down so that Bert could take the car keys. I ended up with the dry heaves in his Mother's front yard. Swearing at all these 'friends" I vowed never to see them again. I called them "wimps" and assholes". Losing friends is not pleasant.

By 3am my Dad came to pick me up because of complaints by the neighbors and because Bert's mom had called him. Popularity – which was so important to me – fell dramatically. I was willing to make my compatriots look bad. I was disgusted with myself, took it out on others, and instead of respecting as friends do, I withdrew into a grumpy self. Alcohol took the best of me.

Years later when there was too much bilirubin in my urine, I realized that I had been giving myself chemical shock treatment with alcohol. This was not the self-medication I had been seeking, because true self medication is almost always impossible to achieve. My mental symptoms of paranoia, agitation and psychosis, were never relieved by any chemical other than those that a psychiatrist could give and even may of those drugs exacerbated the condition. Later in my life sobriety helped me, but it did not ease my mental problems.

Also, in the past scene I became intoxicated with power. In a negative way, I wished to have no part of my friends, imitated an "image", and put virtually everyone down. No wonder I fell so badly. I have crossed the lines of chemicals, mental-emotional reactions, and myths. How responsible am I towards my future? I need an attitude that is positive and optimistic, but versed in reality. I need to keep changing in life.

Late in the 1990's I had many walks with Dad. In its own way this one was remembered.

146

Throughout the years my Dad has kept a watchful eye over me yet let me have freedom. For the most part we have always been able to talk. In a walk around his neighborhood he asked me,

"Have you ever told anyone of late that you are a recovering alcoholic?"

I responded, "No, Dad, everyone I told in the past, scatters like cockroaches when the lights are turned on. I don't need friends like that."

"Well it has been fifteen years since your last drink hasn't it?" he said in a probing way.

"Yes, thanks for remembering."

"What made you want to quit anyways? Surely not me?" he said.

"No Dad, it wasn't you. It was something else. It was the promise that I'd never go into a mental hospital again. And, even though this did not exactly come true it has lead me to places I have never been – and given me so much hope for the future." I sincerely stated.

Curiously he replied, "What made you start drinking in the first place?"

"Bravado – to feel important…the allure of something magical – the bright eyes of the girl in my love life – pretending the girl felt the same way." I continued, "Communications or something of the like --- hot nights – escaping to Never-never land -- to aid in digestion – to wash my system out."

Still quizzing he went on, "You found these things didn't come true?"

"I found they were all transient," I said as if I were failing.

Pointedly Dad asked the question he wanted to ask. "Is all of this enough to keep you from drinking today?"

"Yes," I responded, "In an inverse sort of way. I use images and thoughts to keep me from 'picking up' alcohol today. This includes all drugs and alcohol."

"What are some of these images and thoughts?"

"Well, vomit, the shakes, and gas pain… headaches, and by that I mean all over my body. Brown urine, brown sheets, brown collars, bleary mornings, dreary afternoons, the smell of socks in the hampers at detox – my sex life – my love life – potential friends and lovers leaving – hurtful arguments and fevers that won't quit, and of course, John Wayne."

"John Wayne!"? Dad said incredulously.

"Yes John Wayne, in the flip flop of my values, though John Wayne remains humorous, he is the opposite of what I want. In no way do I want to be like or have the image of a hard living, woman grabbing, bottle sucking, meat eating macho man stud. OK, now and then I will eat a steak, but you get the picture. In no way do I have to believe that satisfaction in life comes to men who swing like a loosely tied ship's boom in a hurricane. Recklessness is out – caution is in. I should have followed your example years ago." With relief I would have continued, but I waited for a response from Dad.

After hesitating for a few seconds Dad made a statement. He spoke slowly, "Don't say that. We all have our own road in life." He was looking at our shoes on the pavement.

"Unfortunately my road has mental hospitals on it. Every time I'm given a new pharmaceutical drug I seem to go into the hospital. I ask you, when will it stop?"

"It will, I believe it will because that is exactly my point. Mother and I never felt that you were that bad. We just thought that you were sick. You know, mentally sick." As he changed the subject I know I had to let him make his point.

Cringing inside I had to go on. "And when did you think this occurred?"

Dad replied, "When the psychosis first occurred – when you were twenty."

I said with force," Just like that? You say it came all at once?"

"Well – give or take a couple months."

I knew Dad's point. He was trying to say that psychosis came over me like a virus or plague. Perhaps it could be by demonic possession or some other foreign factor. He did not see changes in me during my youth he did not want me blaming my parents in the future. Even to admit a genetic problem to him would be admitting a weakness. For some that is too much to ask.

But I continued, "I'm sorry but in this conversation I must be missing something – or actually you are missing something. John Wayne, humorous figure or not, -- I *loved* alcohol long before psychosis came."

Benignly smiling Dad said, "No, *we know* we didn't raise you like that. Don't get me wrong – it's a good thing to stop drinking but you cannot be an alcoholic because you are schizoaffective."

"Your logic is *so* screwed up."

"Oh! How so? We didn't raise you to be an alcoholic. I know that."

"I can't think of a better reason to drink alcohol or use drugs than to be *schizoaffective bipolar.* I'll bet someone tells those damned doctors the same message. Not only is our brain chemistry messed up, but between our own tendency to abuse substances and the medical professions propensity to throw chemicals in our systems no wonder no one gets anywhere but in a pickle jar."

"Remember Bob, "Dad said, "You are mentally ill, first."

Regaining my composure I said to him, "No, you didn't do anything, if that's the way you want to think."

So once again I am to put up with another's opinion. Unfortunately this time it comes from a man whom I've always respected and sometimes emulated – Dad. I hurt only out of pride and the fact that I am told of my limiting disease. At least I don't suspect too much backroom stigma especially from those who can only mumble behind my back. Dad told me what he felt to my face. That man is grateful for gaining his version of the truth. So is this man.

Just two afterthoughts:

(1) If a physician had told me that I would have to stop using alcohol and if it were done at the wrong time in my life, then I would have never quit drinking and most likely would be dead by now.

(2) It should be known that I also have pushed other physical abuse to the back of my mind which was not always remembered in my conscious. My mental illness could therefore be attributed to abuse that had not been dealt with in my mind. Denial is truly an issue.

FOUR

PSYCHIATRIC MANIPULATION

One of the purposes of this book is to show that mentally ill people are not simple minded waif's, not dangerous, do not falsely engender abounding sympathy, and can adjust to and add to society. This writing also shows that treatment (including medicines) can exacerbate problems in these individuals.

Mental patients go through a pain unlike anyone else. They feel alone and isolated and can "act out" as bad as any. The struggle to recover can be long and arduous. First, if medicine should be used it should be chosen wisely with forethought on the patient not on what either the patient or doctor demands. Should there be any reaction to the medicine it should be discontinued even if there is nothing to replace it with. Secondly, the patient must be taught alternative ways to live and adjust in the world around him. Building confidence is more important that strict rules unless there is violence. The struggle to recover becomes easier when it is owned by the patient. Making the patient aware of the present plight or situation is helpful to bring responsibility. In my case, the successful psychiatrists had this attitude towards me. They gave me the benefit of the doubt and allowed me to play a role in my treatment.

The fear I had in the past haunted me until I became older. I became aware that there were other people involved than just the psychiatrist. In my mind I had to deal with their behavior just as they felt my behavior had to be dealt with. The following paragraphs were written in 1993.

"My irrational fear has been lessened to milder anxiety because of the aging process and some real success. I have been successful because my fear is purging out of me. Instead of the mad getting madder, the mad is getting softer. Years ago I felt the lonely pain of a desperate man and would scream in cars, offices, and homes in vain. I have walked miles at night with suitcases and backpacks yelling at lamp posts and mailboxes. I have cried bitter tears for you and for me in utter despair. Now I enthusiastically hug friends and relatives and look into mirror at myself only to weep with joy. I continue to cry in theaters where others may or may not have tears. The intense emotion is built up as a flexed muscle for its next use, but it is changed now and can be lessened instead f needing an outside limiting factor to stop it. Passion comes out in other ways. Animals wag their tails at me, children smile, and babies return my winks and blinks. Sometime in a quiet moment all of a sudden the little man in me gives a hearty laugh and tension is released in a joking way."

Not everyone can understand these mood swings. Other professionals such as aides, nurses, social worker, police, and lawyers who deal with the mentally ill sometimes let *their* own moods get in the way as well. Read this next paragraph, please.

"Police and their squad cars are the first limit one will find for the passionately mentally ill. These, plus handcuff's, quickly quell the emotionally charged patients as they go for a stay at the state hospital. There, big men with crew cuts are employed as security to push around those who come with handcuffs. Just between you and me these are the sickest of the sick because they unfairly wrestle those with handcuff's to the ground and pin their egos as the peaceful are pushed around. Unfortunately there are other limits; those who tie one down in a quiet room, doctors who prescribe ten times the amount of medicine to which one is accustomed, and nurses who tickle the bottom of your feet once you are tied down."

Do we always have to act out our feelings and emotions? The whole game at the hospital is one of dominance enforced by force. There is no way out of it. It becomes even more dangerous when all men are seen as monkeys and powerful psychotropic medicines are present.

Let's look at some of the treatment given to me in the fall of 1979.

With no forewarning a previous doctor refused to renew my prescription for stelazine. As a result I ran out, had a psychotic "break" (inappropriate behavior) in front of a girlfriend's family and lost the young woman as a possible "love".

Since I had to get another medicine in my system fast, I found a new psychiatrist in Dr. Munchken. She was in her mid-fifties and comely.

Dr. Munchken said, "I can't give you stelazine because you can't tell me what to do and because your past doctor took you off of it. Besides you are so depressed over the loss of this girl – too much to be sure."

Frantically I said, "Just give me something that'll work like a phenothiazine, like stelazine, and at least talk to one of my previous psychiatrists."

"No, she said, but here's what I'll do. I'll give you the medicine you want and even better; you come into hospital so I can watch you."

I knew any medicine supplies I had at home were dwindling and I knew I would need help soon. Even though I did not care for the doctor's hubris and felt she was misleading me I said "yes" to her personal moneymaking scheme of putting me in the hospital.

Two Weeks Later

She gave me Triavil and extra doses of valium instead of a simple dose of a phenothiazine. Triavil is three medicines in one; valium, low does phenothiazine, and an antidepressant. In the hospital I became agitated and did odd things. I would call for lost pets from reading in the newspaper and say I was the true owner. I believed people were following me especially as I drove past the old girlfriend's house on passes. Finally I cut my wrists in my own hospital room.

In my pain I began taunting the staff and talking of the doctor's incompetence. Instead of admitting her mistake and giving me the medicine I needed she became more convinced that valium and an antidepressant were just right for me. Honestly, with that medicine in me (and I only speak for myself) I knew something was drastically wrong. Someone should have let me grieve the loss of the girlfriend instead of pumping me up with pills.

As a result I refused all medicine for one day. A security guard chased me around the lunch tables and the doctor called the police. At ten o'clock at night twelve Wilmington policemen dragged me to the state hospital. Later the cops told me that twelve of them were sent just to make the security guard look good. I was not supposed to tell anyone. You know, being moved from hospital to hospital – especially when my brain is full of chemicals – feels like a swirling flush.

I went into this private hospital with trepidation and hope, felt the churning hot flashes of antidepressants and valium, and came out a grumbling waif. Believe me; I did not do this alone. It is the medical profession's arrogance when dealing with patients that prevents acceptance of input – and this is true even when patients are talking about themselves truthfully.

Things did not really change for me in 1993 when I went to another location.

I was at the state hospital where diagnostic procedures are grueling for patients and treatment is scarce.

Seemingly at a random time I was called in an open office where twelve staff members sat watching me. They had me sit on a nearby stool facing each of them. I did not even have time to wash my face or change my shirt. I felt like a "caught" boy going to the principal's office.

"Do you know why you are here?" said an imposing male nurse.

"I am here to be diagnosed by you," I said.

"We already know you and most of us can diagnose you. We want to know what to do with you." said the voice.

Taking my chance I replied, "You don't have to do anything with me – just let me go home."

He said, "What makes you so sure we should?"

"I have a place to live and a wife at that home."

"We don't think you'll be dangerous to her or yourself – but is there anyone else?"

"No one I can think of. There may be resentments toward others but I can work my way through those."

The mail nurse thought for a minute and changed tact, "Call them what you wish, but I have a question for you."

"OK", I replied waiting for his test.

Carefully I heard the words, "Do you hear voices that make you move."

Slowly, I said, "What do you mean by 'voices'?"

"You know what I mean," he said

"You mean do I hear voice in my head where I feel a compulsion to follow."

"Right," he said with relief.

"No, No, way."

"I don't believe you – I have that right you know." he challenged.

I responded, "You have a right to believe whatever you want, and I have the right to tell the truth – regardless of how you feel."

"So you lie too," he prodded.

"I'm not lying right now." I retorted

"Then how do you explain it?" he queried

I answered with a question; half of me expecting him to get angry with me. "Explain what?"

The room was quiet – it seemed that the male nurse and I were the only ones present. He looked at me and with direct eyes said, "Explain you behavior right here, now."

I thought of the present and said. "I am sitting on this stool, talking to you, thinking of my schizoaffective bipolar type diagnosis and wondering what you are going to do with me."

"DING DONG! DING DONG!" a bell went off in the wall.

"Apparently someone likes what I said," I sarcastically mused.

"Why did you say that?" The nurse went on trying to sound sincere.

"Don't try to fool me. I've been here enough times to know one of you controls the sounds in the wall. Do you want me to show you the hidden speakers which drive patients insane? The entire hospital is made strangely. At night even in far off rooms with the doors closed you can here voices from the nurse's station. You ask us all if we 'hear' voices. Get lost, this is built in insanity." I then waited for his response.

The nurse was stern, "That 'Get lost' I heard."

"OK, I'm sorry – but I can't say that this hospital is one that engenders trust."

[Because of that "Get lost" I believe I was kept on a different ward for three more weeks. Perhaps I cause my own pain – and you know what is even more painful – the hospital may have been right in doing it].

"Mr. Franz," a dignified older male voice with an Indian accent said, "I want to break this up now and you are to go with Dr. Mobitar. I just want to say to everyone that this hospital many not be here to 'engender trust' but more to fulfill a mission. Let's all work for that."

Dr. Mobitar was an Indian woman who was probably a little younger than me. Her eyes were deep brown and pierced me if they were not focused in a darting manner. She gave me a full twenty minutes of her time and kept drilling me as to why "I did not admit" to hearing voices. Where I was complimented that she would spend so much time with me, I resented her thought that I was really sick. Finally she asked, "Would you like a pass to go home for the weekend?"

With inside glee I said quietly, "That would be nice," and decided not to get sarcastic about the voices. I know cooperation was necessary when something was offered, even if I thought I should be out on my own.

Two days later after I had made plans to go on a pass with my family a nurse came to me and asked me to take some medicine. She said it was optional before I went on my pass. I graciously declined. Dr. Mobitar quickly beat a path to me.

"You are not going on a pass today." She said angrily.

"Why?" said I just as angry.

"Because you are not doing everything I need you to do. You did not take my medicine." Just then two attendants grabbed my arms and pulled me away from her and down the hall. I yelled – loudly, "I'm not going to swear, but I am sick of it. You are just full of puff, fluff, and other stuff! Quit doing this. Your moodiness is worse than the patients."

With that, in the course of a long minute, another kindly nurse gave me a shot to drink of I-don't-know-what. I went out on a weekend pass with my family.

Relying on other people's decisions in my life is difficult because they can be forced or coerced. Whether it is good or bad medicine contrived consequences are presented.

154

Why can't there be an initial discussion, or at least an explanation? This hubris or arrogance makes a patient an object.

The truth of the matter is that I could have hit someone with my fist. I had enough aggression. Perhaps if this whole scenario played out in a different way I would never realize my denial. Then again if I had let any aggression show whatsoever in those last three weeks I may not have the same living situation I have now. Living at the state hospital means that one must protect yourself at all times or else have the corn bread on your plate stolen by someone else. Rarely does one see compassion for others or for self.

This time was difficult for Leslie Jeanne as well. I needed to realize that her circumstances and co-dependency were affecting her health as well. It was difficult to see that to help her I had to learn how to discipline my own self-care.

"So Mr. Ted E. Bear," said Leslie Jeanne. "What can you say about the past two examples?"

"A patient better watch out for a show of aggression. Even perceived aggression --- maybe the way he walks or talks – can get him into trouble. Yes, do not act too strong even if it is needed with others. This is difficult when one is amidst confined, unhappy people who stand around looking at each other with nowhere else to go but to face another unstable person. Even so, in the second example the State Hospital was well to keep me another three weeks because I was so worn out (or worn through) I could have hit someone.

All of this I feel was built up throughout the years. The continued changing of medicine from doctor to doctor exhausted me. (I react to antidepressants and any addictive drug such as xanax or valium in an aggressive way). At that time I had depressive-aggression. In short, the medical profession had lost all my trust."

"Bob, we will continue this discussion later," continued Leslie Jeanne, "You just need more rest."

FIVE

STIGMA

"The next two chapters are written as if they were collages." Ted E. Bear said.

"What do you mean?" ask Teribear

"Each is a series of facts or opinions that enhances the stories within. I admit it isn't eloquent writing but it is the best I could do at the time. You have to realize, Teribear, that at times I do not do well mentally and my writing suffers. When I am not tense about a subject, and feel loose I can write proficiently. You should see this in the book – it part of my illness. The chapter on 'Stigma' made me nervous more so than the chapter on 'Recommendation's."

Teribear thought a moment as said, "Do you have all your faculties now?"

"Some would say no, but I think so," Ted E. Bear replied.

"I definitely have faith in you, my beary-bear friend," she stated with reason.

As much as I give the psychiatrists criticism, I remain very loyal to them for when no one else will defend mentally ill people, they will. I am not only speaking in those isolated cases of violence by mentally ill people where doctors are called upon to make a case for the 'defendants' but I am speaking of stigma that comes our way each and every day. Most people perpetuate this stigma even though, according to the Mental Health Association in Delaware, one fifth of our current population takes medicine for mental or emotional needs. Even psychiatrists get stigma leveled at them for just treating the chronically mentally ill. According to one source threats have come to a doctor because of treating paranoid schizophrenic persons.

Stigma is prejudice directed toward mentally ill people. In the English language there are a myriad of derogatory words that serve this cause. From the words "anal" and "asinine" to "zealot" and "zoo-dweller," English words describe the ill colorfully with twists to the negative. We see in television programming the line. "Did you take your lithium today?" said in the condescending way where one actor shows dominance over the next by acting as if people who take medicine are unstable. We can see it in political cartoons all over the nation. If you would have treated the mentally challenged the same way you have treated the mentally diseased, then you would have been sued or ruined. I mean it.

In 1993 I applied for a job at a local steakhouse. This scene I call "Steakhouse Blues."

"Hmm, I can see there are some discrepancies in your job history," said the steakhouse restaurant manager.

"What do you mean?" said I.

"I mean gaps in your work history," he said, "What do you make of that?"

"Well, sometimes I have to work and sometimes I don't have to."

"According to me, one has to work all the time, Isn't that right?"

Resigned I said, "No, it's not always necessary to work all the time."

"Let me try a different tact," he replied "Look at that last job you had. Was that a real job, being a 'Co-Director to a Drop-In Center', or was it just a made-up gig for you to get paid?"

"It was a real job where I helped edit a newsletter and organized and went on activities with Mental Health Consumers." I replied trying not to get angry.

"And you, too, are one of these 'mental health consumers'?"

"Yes," I said reluctantly.

"Tell me, what is wrong with you?"

"I don't feel comfortable right now."

"You either tell me or I call the police, right now."

"What do you want to call the police for? If you have to know then I will say I am manic depressive."

"Then I will tell them that I have a manic depressive here that is bothering me, and they'll come take you away. How would you like that?"

"The Americans with Disabilities Act will help me."

"The American with Disabilities Act will help me! It was meant for me the employer not you, the job applicant. You're just the type we don't want working at this Steakhouse. Unless you tell me all about your medicines, and I know there are more than one, then goodbye and good riddance."

So I said rather tersely, "That's where I get off, with that attitude of demanding to know my personal business; I say good riddance to you."

As it happened, by the time I drove home, the police were calling me. I convinced them over the phone that I was on a job interview, which was true, and that the prospective employer was not desirable to work for because he did not respect the A.D.A. I also had to tell them that I did not overturn tables and chairs as I was so accused. Later that day, I received a call offering me a job at the steakhouse and without regret I did not accept it.

Was this prospective employer stigmatized? Was *he* actually another mental health consumer? These are the questions I have to answer. It is true that how one has been treated is how one treats others. One-fifth of the population that takes medication is actually prescribed four or five strong medications. Compare that to those who take one medicine PRN (as needed). So there is an echelon or strata of clients where one could look down on another. I hate to say it, but even I show stigma to others, perhaps unconsciously. When I see mental pathology, either due to sickness or side effects from medicine, I visibly become uncomfortable because I identify with that person. If the person's knee is shaking, -- then so will mine. When a person constantly rubs their head then so will I wish to do also just for the sake of imitation. It all comes down to me just wanting to walk away. In the true story of "Steakhouse Blues" I did walk away using the same works he used to me – "Good Riddance". As a result, I try to hide out with "normal" people and abhor going into hospitals.

Looking at the actual need to take medicine for the brain – the hypothalamus – also seems foreign to me. Some species of rodents have a gland that makes Vitamin C which is not produced in humans. We have to be dependent on our eating habits or actually take pills of Vitamin C. I am not proposing genetic research to make a synthetic gland to produce Thorazine or Lithium Carbonate, but instead wonder just what genetic manipulations are possible. The Japanese are rapidly isolating a human gene for schizophrenia and are inserting clusters of genetic material into human genes. I cannot be certain how ethical considerations are being handled, but one thing is certain – there will be a plethora of information about medicines in the coming years and we should pay attention. Needing an outside chemical could be the norm for most of the population. What do we say about stigma toward people who take medicines then? Will the medicines be as needed as vitamins?

In late 1991, when I worked at detox, I overheard a conversation between a Delaware State Trooper and a Wilmington Policeman. The policeman asked the trooper how he could determine which subject in a domestic squabble has to leave the house if they both take medicine and are in the middle of a disagreement. Without much thought the

158

trooper said that the person who takes the most medicine must leave the house in a domestic quarrel. This means the most number of medicines, and not the amount of the medicine. I've often wondered how cops make their decisions. How can you expect a cop to know all of the in's and out's of medicine? I can see why to make it simple? In some cases these techniques could perpetuate stigma. I'll just keep my medicine cabinet locked.

After initial steps were taken by me towards recovery in 1997 I attended a church service where some "helpful" people wanted me to stop taking my medicine. I ran into a man at a church and after a thirty minute conversation he questioned me as to why I was seeing a psychiatrist. Then he told me that I did not need medicine and that I should stop taking it. At a younger age I might have bit the hook. Now I just call these people "old farts." Why is it so important to him that I don't take any medicine? What business is it of his? Furthermore, a Catholic priest at one time went to one of my psychiatrists and told her that I did not belong on medicine. The psychiatrist heeded his advice and took me off medicine. Within a few days I was roaming the New York country side, ditching my car to look for work as a "hired hand" in the Tarrytown suburbs. For a long while I had amnesia and could not recall my name.

For my adult life I have needed certain medicines that work in my system. Substituting others doesn't always work and such experiments fail in disaster. Why do others continue to pester me with what they want? – That I should get off meds. There must be some need for them to tamper with others' lives. I think that they just want to be important, and those are the kind of people that really aren't needed by me. In short, when I am off meds I become non-communicative and angry – just ask Leslie Jeanne. Without medications behavior is aberrant; with medications are side effects and others' opinions. No wonder the mentally ill like privacy. Frankly, now, if I had the 'balls', I would never have put up with this shit from others at all.

Listed are reasons why some other people tell me to get off medicine. To me, none of these are valid.

REASONS TO GET OFF MEDS (According to Passersby's):

- like to criticize

- they fear having someone tell them to take meds.

- cannot differentiate between medicine and street drugs

- unable to diagnose me because I became so "normal".

- frustrated that they aren't more effective in life.

- wish to "convert" others

- have resentments towards medical doctors

- do not understand the medicine

- think what's good for them is good for everybody else

- misery loves company

When I come across these people I let them talk themselves out, say a work of thanks, and go about my business. Perhaps I should show them this list. Know-it-alls "hang out" around every true discipline.

To me it seems that in the second half of the twentieth century mental patients are the most studied group in the world. After all haven't we taken the role of a captive audience by not being involved in the direction of our future? We either "follow nicely" or individually put up a big fight in the struggle of dependence or independence. Perhaps because of the disability of individual false pride are mental patients unable to work together. We are too concerned about our individual lives.

All around this country studies are done in mental wards. For the most part the patients have no idea of what is happening. It is natural to use this population for study because hospitals are contained environments and subjects are captive. The scene is seen as a true microcosm of society. One can study (falsely or not) anthropology, sociology, or psychology on the mental ward. All of this is in the controlled environment of the doctors. It's too bad that I thought I would get well in these places. Haven't you ever noticed they keep you as long as your insurance will pay? What a racket.

Early in my treatment I watched others and made decisions affecting my future.

In an expensive Philadelphia Mental Institution a number of years ago I met a married young woman who was schizophrenic and pregnant. This meant that she could not take the medicine necessary to treat her schizophrenia. Each day her husband came to visit as she looked forward to being with loved ones. From what I understood the woman was able to function moderately outside of the hospital for about a month after she became pregnant, but subsequently had to live in the hospital for approximately eight months or until she could be titrated on medicine again. In all of her schizophrenic thought and movement she never lost sight of the fact that she was pregnant. In fact, the couple had planned this baby from conception. I say this to show that "normal" functioning can be approached by schizophrenic pregnant women.

Much as I love children. I have decided that I do not want to father any. The reason for this is that I do not want to see my children go through the literal hell that I have gone through. Even if they had the best care possible it would not stop me from feeling this way. I definitely believe that the illness I have is heredity based and that my children would not be comfortable in this world as it is. I don't care what you think. Why father children when you are convinced life would be miserable for them? Even animals don't make love when it is not safe – unless you are a rabbit. Slowly, as I get older I learn my limitations.

My Dad had been involved in finding housing for the mentally ill. Patients have remembered him in Wilmington and he has cared for these people. Primarily he worked for the Alliance for the Mentally Ill (NAMI-Delaware). In his work he had to speak to neighbors of consumers to see how they felt about having the mentally ill live next door. Even now, I am told, people generally understand and the consumers are welcomed, but every now and then someone puts up a fuss. The big cry is, "Not in my backyard," which means its fine for others, but not for this neighborhood. In these cases the neighbor's behavior is based on some sort of fear. Safety or financial fears are the most common which are quelled readily by discussion, but every now and then human nature begins 'looking down' on others instead of giving compassion. In actuality this is a fear, as well, which shows a lack of education about mentally ill people and in an ignorant way turns into hate. When I first saw this hate for my kind I became fearful and wanted to fight back. Now I just walk away and say "You do not have all the facts."

Mental health consumers are organizing on a grass roots level. Unfortunately, they have been trying to do this for a long time and it is slow going. Also, apathy from that one fifth of the population who takes medicine does not help the organization. With a wide array of diagnoses the group runs into complications and stops. We still rely on what other people can do for us, regrettably, and information leaks out before it can be used properly.

Take for example the diagnoses which I mentioned before. A diagnosis is a tool used by physicians to denote what treatment is needed for each individual afflicted with the disease. Bipolar, unipolar, manic depression, schizoaffective, and schizophrenia all denote separate conditions which receive different treatments and medicine. To have these professional words brought out to the public makes them labels. Now every comedian under the sun will again pick on my diagnosis as a snotty kid would take his finger to his nose. Furthermore, if any person is a combination of these disorders they would get hit twice or more and need to find even thicker skin. I realize that only four out of one hundred people in this country are majorly mentally ill, but don't minorities still have rights?

Other information must be taught as well. For example, people should learn to be responsible for their own behavior. First, we never should use a diagnosis or "label" to excuse illegal or immoral behavior. Second, we must realize that with each individual's ability to change – even if it is just by changing a habit – personal mettle solidifies. If it is necessary, find a higher authority to help, then seek one out. Should a person then find a need for a chemical or drug, then seek the help of the medical profession not another "helpful advisor". We answer to our behavior wherever we go, and no matter who we are – we are responsible.

The aforementioned words have universal application. To a student of mental illness it means to be prepared if illness strikes in your own family. To a mentally ill individual this responsibility means that not only must one learn how to cope adequately in life, but that it is more important to change within the bounds of decency; I for one believe this can be accomplished.

When I worked as a Co-Director for a center for the mentally ill I interfaced with others in the public who were also helping people. Here I write about meeting a fellow traveler in the field of mental health:

Today I just came from a meeting at the Alliance for the Mentally Ill in Delaware and met Mr. Dick Johnson from AARP. Mr. Johnson would not admit to having ever heard of the common diagnoses, yet I know he had heard them before in other meetings and conferences. His point was to say that the medical professionals treat most mentally ill primarily from symptoms with medications that are symptom based. Very rarely does one find a pure schizophrenic or a pure bipolar or the like. As a result medicines are prescribed by physicians based on what behaviors are displayed.

It was Mr. Johnson's contention that many of the elderly show symptoms that crossover different diseases and they are never diagnosed in a direct way, therefore the elderly are stigmatized in this way. Schizophrenia, dementia, senility, bipolar and Alzheimer's, all turn out to be the same thing in the elderly according to a few professionals. Medicines are then given for individual symptoms regardless of the side effects. There is not real care and this is just another form of discrimination.

Back to the point; give people responsibility for themselves, and more often than not, they will seek to live up to it. To do this it may be necessary to give information so that they can at least seek help, but personal responsibility can be achieved especially with the powerless if they are given the chance.

Here is just a word about medicine:

The medicine to help mentally ill people is just not available yet. There is not medicine that solves basic biochemical needs of the individual.

Instead, we get medicines which treat symptoms and have many side effects. We get class after class of these medicines pushed on doctors and patients without coming to a true biochemical answer. How long will this last? When will we get true definitions and answers? I feel that comes only with patience and persistence.

When I have worked with the elderly I noticed that most of them, even in the final stages of life, remain attached to their caregivers. This is true even if it is impossible to remember names. The patients I cared for always knew me and were ready for each successive activity. If dementia was the issue and the person could not look up into my face, then they knew my touch and would allow me to at least comfortably change their position.

This is in contrast to the state hospital where younger adults dwell. In these cases, for example, a patient can make a commotion with many foul words to the point where the staff reacts angrily. The staff *reacts* instead of *responds*, and everything becomes an emotional struggle instead of a learning experience. Punitive action is taken and the rules become punishment instead of consequences. As a result the professional become emotional and the situation is a tug-of-war of strength instead of a lesson to be learned. Wouldn't it be easier to first explain the rules and then if they weren't consistently followed have the patient go to the quiet room or seclusion room with no staff yelling or carrying on? It is not with dignity that the mentally ill are graciously maligned.

I would like to make a further point by reporting something from CNN Headline News (6/11/97) which showed ten year old children learning how to act from actors in the field. The actors were instructed to just talk to the children normally and to not show exaggerated emotions. As a result, all of the children learned how to act very well, without the use of hyperbole emotion. This proves, to me, that people can learn how to behave (act) without the use of exaggeration, histrionics, or any other strong emotion leveled at them. It is a moot point to say, but "monkey do what monkey see". At any age – with or without mental illness – this is true. Therefore the biggest problem in treatment may not be all the reactions of the ill, but counter-reactions of the professional themselves.

A problem with some patients and consumers which I have been dealing with for a very long time is known as "terminal uniqueness," and it causes isolation, loneliness, egotism, selfishness, self-pity and low self-esteem. "Terminal uniqueness" means that one feels *so* different from other people that in most ways the patient is unknowingly harming himself with self-centeredness. Unless one finds a way to move towards others then one will continue moving inwards. It moves to the point where other people become objects and the biggest friend and companion is directly off the television, video game or another inanimate distraction. Stigma has then turned inwards as it rears its ugly head as a scene from To Kill a Mockingbird. We just don't know who to trust and lashing out is possible.

Certainly, the judgments of the staff are received by patients as stigma for it is easy to isolate into terminal uniqueness. Stigma is real and it needs to be prevented. Each individual in the public, on the hospital staff, and as a patient has got to stop thinking solely just about themselves. The next account is an example of each individual having a personal self-centered agenda. This occurrence happened in a department store while I was at work as a sales associate.

I had observed Ephrem on the street and in two institutions prior to this meeting and although he could not remember my name we both recognized each other. When I spied him shopping, I at first felt an uncomfortable tenseness in fear that he would be like other consumers and make a big fuss over me. Now that the Christmas season was over, and there weren't so many customers, I could pay more attention to him. I had job as a Sales Associate in a well known Philadelphia department store.

Ephrem was clean, and appeared sober. I did not detect an odor and his dark blue clothes set him apart from the crowd, along with his deep colored complexion. He always wore a ski-cap dark in color and shiny black boots – even in the summer. Rarely would he talk and it was always in a low mumble. Strangely enough, I was glad to see him but I had to keep that a secret.

"Look at that despicable bum," said Chip, "he makes this place look bad – I mean real bad." Chip Monke had graduated from high school a year before and spent some months working in the candy department. "Have you ever smelled him? He's got this terrible smell that won't quit. Someone should just lock him away."

"Oh, I know his type just from looking at him," Binda replied, "He shouldn't be out now. It's mealtime at Farnhurst." Binda was a part time substitute teacher when she wasn't working at the department store. "If he came close to any of my kids I'd have him put in jail."

"Don't they feed him in that place, Binda? Every time I see him in the candy department he's either asking for a sample or a handout." Following that statement Chip Monke laughed so hard that he had to lay on the floor right next to men's socks. "What a disgrace!" and he laughed some more after taking another breath.

"Look," said Binda, "He's trying on a cowboy hat."

"Oh, shit," muttered Chip, "What's become of this men's department? – Bob? Aren't you going to say anything?"

I quietly said, "No, because I know what he does."

"What?" they both seemed to answer incredulously "What do you mean?"

By this time I could not hold back from talking. I was angry and laughing at the same time. Things just did not seem to matter and Ephrem was coming to the register with two pairs of pants, a long sleeve shirt, a belt and the cowboy hat. I looked at Chip Monke and Binda and said:

"This guy puts all these goods on layaway at the beginning of each month and as he goes through the month he 'returns' the items for the money he has put down. It is a form of banking since it is so difficult to get to the bank or even an ATM machine. If anything is left over he keeps it."

"You probably told him to do that." Binda said.

"No," I said.

"Yes, but you know him, I know you know him. Where have you been Bob? Just where have you been Bob?"

And so it goes, and so it goes, and so it went – anonymity that is. Not only mine but everyone involved. When a change is needed some may have to feel discomfort. "I'm sorry, I really am sorry, I apologize." Perhaps someday it will not be necessary to be so secretive.

What I desire is what I have to give. Willingness is the key and forgiveness is the lock. To use these two qualities takes courage and persistence. May we be led in this nation to rid ourselves of stigma towards persons with mental and emotional illnesses? The answer is a resounding affirmative. Education is necessary if we are to have peace, then dignity will come.

Here are some other thoughts:

© 1997 Gary Brookin – North America Syndicate

Most often creators of editorial cartoons are insightful, humorous and brave. They can speak where others will not or do not.

In this case they describe in a humorous way just how the majority of mental health patients have been looked at in the late 20th century. Their purpose is to create humor so that all of us can and will look to reduce the stigma which has been perpetuated onto the mentally ill. The exaggerations make us laugh.

Through this freedom of laughter we can find ways of accepting all of us back into society. The cartoons serve as positive examples of just how our ownership of exaggeration moves us to a beginning of accepting each and every one of us into a realm of society where we all can be useful.

Thank you for listening and viewing these thoughts.

SIX

RECOMMENDATIONS

The purpose of this chapter is to make some recommendations to the medical and legal professions who interface with mental health consumers, and to clients who are willing to do the work necessary to stay well.

I have mentioned in earlier chapters how doctors are possessive towards clients, how doctors demand obedience from clients, especially in terms of medicine and how clients are treated in clinics and continuous treatment teams (CTTs), along with how the police treat clients. In my humble option (if I have one), friction and strife need to be lessened.

I have listed my recommendations (as a professional in my field) for the medical profession, the legal profession, and mental health consumers and clients.

The Medical Profession:

To the psychiatrists:

In my view the most important quality you medical professionals have should be to take care of yourselves. You must be healthy. I heard Dr. Kay Redfield Jamison speak recently about her battle with manic depression in a speech entitled "Passages of a Wounded Healer." Not only did she tell her story but she told the audience that she personally knew of at least one hundred fifty other doctors who were also manic depressive. Doctors cannot heal others adequately until they help themselves. This is why the end of this chapter is so important – to a point one can be his own client. I feel that you and other medical professionals) should treat yourselves a recovering alcoholics who attend Al-Anon. By this I mean, that just as recovering alcoholics do not drink, you should do everything possible to keep your mental health. Also, the reason a particular recovering alcoholic goes to Al-Anon is to keep centered in the face of turmoil from his friends and family. You have to keep centered as well, in the face of all of your patients and families.

One of Al-Anon's basic tenets is to "detach with love" and this means that when people and things are crazy and confusing around you, then it's time to pull away into self and do nothing but have regard for those who are causing the confusion. In this way the responsibility for the confusion lies with those who created it in the first place. Remember, people come to you for help. You have your limits. How much can you really control someone else's life? Once you've done what you can there is no more to offer. Besides, it would most likely help the client to solve his own problems instead of relying on someone else.

Other suggestions to you have to do with all clients and not just the mentally ill. Please, speak to the clients, and try to have the client build a relationship. Those of you who just sit quietly saying nothing appear hostile. The 'quiet stare' some psychiatrists give clients are a feeble attempt of dominance. Are we really that much of an animal? Are you? Dr. Kenneth Weller, of the Institute of Pennsylvania Hospital, told me that to start a relationship and to keep it going, it is necessary to show some interest and concern for the client. In fact, he told me when I was a counselor at the Kirkwood Detox that when in doubt, show concern and the client will be willing to talk more about his life. The whole issue here is about engaging in a relationship. To engage means to "bind by contract" according to Webster's dictionary, and in the therapeutic sense it means to treat the person while you are with them, then move to detachment once you go on to something else.

The issue of control comes up in doctor – client relationships. Ideally the patient (client) will move to control his own life. Before this occurs the doctor must decide just what to do. It is like a differential gear in the relationship because one small statement on the doctor's part may affect a great change in the patient. I once had a psychiatrist who thought I could write; now I am writing a long manuscript hoping it will get published. My current psychiatrist sees me for ten minutes every three weeks. He is very verbal by asking me questions and actually gives advice. I appreciate his honesty – a quality not found in some other psychiatrists I have seen. I trust him that he will not jerk around my medicine as some others have done to me.

This is just for me. I do not trust therapists that seem to work by themselves. I like to know that therapists can work near and with other therapists or in a hospital or clinic setting. This shows humility on the doctor's part in that a client may need a second opinion for himself, or just plain support. It is a comfort when I see psychiatrists and psychologist work in clusters because I feel the strength of many. Those psychiatrists who care for each other have the capacity to care for clients in a healthy way.

To the patients (clients):

First, I want to say that to find a good psychiatrist it may be necessary to look for one. It is possible to interview doctors. Usually though they think this is strange, but really it is a good option. You could have a list of questions and see how the transference is when you first see the doctor. Expect to pay a charge for your first visit as they will look at this as though they were giving a second opinion. The best option is to get a referral from a friend or referral service. A second option is the phonebook. In this way you get to know the doctor and something about him/her. Remember; only by talking with the doctor will you really know whether you should continue to see him/her.

There are other people in the medical profession who can help besides doctors. I probably received the most help from a pharmacist at the local drugstore. This particular pharmacy even has a place for consultation. I receive information on all the medicines I purchase and the pharmacist has a record of every drug I have purchased at that pharmacy. Not only do we talk of drug interaction and side effects, but he gives me information on the diseases or conditions for which they are prescribed.

Nurses and aides are also a good source of information or consultation. Many times when I cannot reach the doctor with an anxious call I can talk to these people and get some relief. Don't get the impression that I'm always calling, however; last year I only called twice in the evening when I found it necessary to ventilate strong emotion. Probably the best thing I ever did for myself was to learn how to express my feelings accurately. This comes from me engaging in conversations with nurses, case managers, counselors, aides and AA. I like to keep lines open and go to them with both the good and the bad. If they always hear the bad – anxiety and complaints – then they will soon tune me out.

I believe that for the most part people who go into the helping professions mean well. It's up to the patient to realize that professionals are human; also, therefore it is necessary for the patient to accept and understand inconsistencies in the profession.

To the Legal Profession:

To attorneys and courts:

Some people believe that our system is not working because the plea of insanity causes many to receive lighter sentences. I believe that all people should be responsible and make restitution for crimes committed.

Let me introduce a plea to you that encourages responsibility and restitution at the same time. It is, "Guilty, but Mentally Ill."

This plea means that the individual knows he did the act and at the time of the action he knew it was wrong. The part of the plea admitting mental illness means that this should be entered into consideration in sentencing. Therefore, his sentencing could be like everyone else and have time in jail or a fine or both. It could, however, be a sentence of restitution. The man would have to pay back to the victims what they've lost. In essence, restitution is tied to the sentence. If a man throws a brick through a window, and he knows he did it, then under this plea the judge could fine him or put him in jail and still make him replace the window. Or, the judge could make him wash windows for a month. Whatever results from the bench in this plea would cause a situation that would be a learning experience for the mentally ill man instead of using just punishment as a deterrent. This is exactly what the mentally ill need – a taste of reality in a learning environment.

To the police:

I've had plenty of experience with the police and I have one question for you. "Why are you so damned suspicious?" You must fear the mentally ill with a passion. I *can* understand a weapons search and the use of handcuffs, but this "good cop," – "bad cop" game you play is nauseating. At least in my ease I will honestly answer your questions. Most mentally ill, as myself for example, do not wish or want others to die or become hurt. Besides if you would use a little more gentility you'd probably find out more.

I have to admit that when I was having problems five years ago I was accosted by three sets of police that did a very good job. They stayed rational and calm and the whole time taking me to the state hospital. The rest of them were too aggressive looking for a bust.

Finally, I've got to say that writing out how one wants to be approached by police can be put on the police computer system. If you look at it before you come and get me you'll know how to approach me. For example I could tell you to have one policeman get on his knees behind me and have another talk to me moving me backward until I trip and fall. Then he could put handcuffs on me, search my person, and search my room. Wouldn't you rather have it that way? Never, do I want to see anyone get hurt.

To the clients (patients):

Whatever you do, try to stay calm and collected. Be honest and responsible. Keep the lines open to communication and open up with significant others. Expect others not to trust you in times of trouble so you will not be surprised when they don't. Remember that you are not alone in your pain. Try not to isolate and if you believe in a God then talk to him. Do not become hurtful to others. If you can, just walk away when anger strikes you. Look for peace.

The rest of this chapter is devoted to mental health as seen by me. Shown here is a mental health schema for assessment which I use. I use this to "check" myself physically, mentally, emotionally, and spiritually. In part, I adopted this way of looking at my being from the 'organizations' of Twelve Step Groups and also Recovery Inc. This is just a framework an individual can use. Any individual can use it from psychiatrist to patient, from judge to jury, and from cop to client. This framework helps me assess myself so that at any given point in time I can relax and know what action to take, if any.

To all:

Periodically I need to assess myself to see what action need to be taken in the future. After all the questions have been answered I then make a judgment of what to do and how to go about doing it. I have divided the questions into categories of physical, mental, emotional, and spiritual qualities. Since these are changeable there are different actions to be taken at different times. You may make up some of your own questions.

Physical

The physical deals with all behavior and functions of the body:

Digestion -- Am I taking my medicine correctly and at the proper time?

Am I drinking enough fluid and taking vitamins?

Is the food I am eating quality food?

Am I eating too much?

Am I not using drugs and alcohol?

Is my elimination regular?

Nervous -- Am I tired most of the time?

Do I show displays of anger?

Does my knee or hand shake uncontrollably?

Is my speech and language appropriate?

How strong is my libido?

Have I been cheating on someone else?

Do I get regular exercise in a routine?

Is my driving within the limits of safety?

Monetarily -- Do I spend too much money?

Do I gamble?

Do I cheat others?

Do I use other people with my money?

Can I save money for future use?

Do I give too much money to charity?

Now that I know approximately where I stand with my behavior I am able to go further and find the root cause – hopefully to eradicate it from my life. The next step is to look at the mental qualities.

Mental

The object of the mental quality is to see what motivates the behavior in the physical quality and to change it if necessary. This should be done in a rational, cognitive way. Questions are as follows:

> Is my behavior due to lust, envy, or greed?
>
> What do I need to stop unhealthy behavior?
>
> What do I need to change in my attitude?
>
> Which feeling best describes my motivation behind unhealthy behavior – fear? anger? love?

If I can be honest in answering these questions, then it is possible to change the motivating force that is causing the behavior. Ideally I should be motivated by love, hence my tendency towards envy would diminish if I could practice love towards those I envied. Most likely this could only happen after talking to another person or journalizing in my journal. Like everything else a change in attitude takes time to grow.

Emotional

For me, the emotional is important when I am not doing well mentally. Instead of thinking things through I go through life recklessly spilling over thoughts into feelings this is especially true in times of psychosis when thoughts are not rational and I become a 'ball' of emotion. It's just too hard to stop the feeling.

I knew an older man who told me he does not like to look at the emotional side because he has a tendency to coddle his feelings thereby spoiling himself to the point of self-pity. In no way do I wish to be in self-pity again so I'll just use the emotion when I am doing particularly poor. The questions are:

> Where is my greatest pain?
>
> Does that pain motivate me?
>
> Am I reacting to that pain?
>
> Are my reactions genuine?
>
> Are my reactions rational?
>
> What do I do when someone hurts me?
>
> Do I see good points in others?
>
> Do I see good points in myself?

Like the mental quality, the object here is to find a motivating force that changes the physical behavior for the better. The emotional component deals with residual feelings which cannot be changed by the cognitive alone.

Spiritual

The spiritual really changes your attitude, and that is what it is meant to do. This 'connection with God' works even if it is a trumped up version of self-hypnosis. You get what you put into it. Let's say that someone is having trouble with fear. Instead of telling them to not be fearful, you offer them faith. If someone else is greedy or full of envy, they are offered the quality of trust. Always in the spiritual realm do we offer a positive to replace the negative. "If it works don't fix it" Questions are as follows:

Do you have faith in anything or anyone?

Do you trust anything or anyone implicitly?

What do you believe about spirits and the universe?

If you can't or won't go to church are you willing to walk into a meadow and look at a lone tree?

Is religion perfect? Is man?

Is religion a reminder of the spiritual world?

Do you use a tickle file?

Once you know your behavior shortcomings are you willing to pray to be rid of them?

If you cannot pray then can you meditate?

Can love be anywhere?

These questions are supposed to raise consciousness about God and the spiritual world. If there is any type of positive response, then the next exercise is more valuable. For two people who already know each other the aforementioned questions need not be asked. My point in mentioning all four qualities – physical, mental, emotional, and spiritual – is that these encompass a total assessment of a human being.

Example: a layperson's "diagnosis"

Leslie Jeanne and I were going out to dinner at a local restaurant and I had an accounting final the next morning. She sensed that I was not feeling very well and asked me what was wrong. I told her that I wasn't very hungry, and that my knee was shaking every time I sat down.

She said, "I've also noticed that you've been smoking and biting your nails. I haven't seen you like this in a long time. Is there anything I can do?"

"You can give me a diagnosis as we used to do when we were dating – and then a plan of action." I said dryly.

When we reached our table in the restaurant she removed a piece of paper from her purse and wrote physical, mental, emotional, and spiritual on the top of four columns on the paper. Then as I talked she wrote each symptom in one of the columns. Under physical she wrote: not hungry, knee shaking, smoking and biting nails. Under mental she wrote: worried, negative attitude. Under emotional she wrote: anticipatory fear, and under spiritual was written: Needs more faith in himself and trust in God.

Leslie Jeanne's diagnosis of me was simple: "Due to outside pressures this patient is suffering from – 'Student Worries'. For this; action must be taken. "Bob, remember that 'this too shall pass' and to 'take it easy.' Remember in the general scheme of things 'how important is it?', and then you should pray for faith and trust."

"I think my attitude is going to change after this final." I said.

"No, it is going to change when you start praying." replied Leslie Jeanne.

"I hope so," I said.

For best results in using the layperson's "diagnosis" another person should do it to you. This provides for a more objective view of what you are going through. Then try it to the other person and you will realize you have an idea plan of action. It is the time given to our brothers and sisters that makes it so special. Also, make sure you write it on paper because the entire scheme becomes more tangible. Whereas paper can be destroyed, but a good plan of action will last a long time.

Epilogue
Summer 2013

I want you to be able to pin American views on mental health to culture in our society through time. In my own life I have pinned down my mental health by controlling the input into my body. For quite some time I have not used or abused alcohol, drugs and smoke products. Please consider these points which are so important:

At the 21st century's turn, the issues of mental health continue to be fronting our society. In early military and western movies John Wayne began his acting. You could say that his film success was a precursor to current "Action" movies. Many viewers believe that Mr., Wayne was type cast in his films. Notice previously that the young Bob wanted to imitate the macho man in the morally questionable imbibing of alcohol.

In fact my teenage negativity made me get lost in a number of areas. Spirituality, alcohol, sex, drugs and rock & roll were in my mind as a tangled web. It was difficult to find a place to stay grounded. In my acceptance of the seriousness of John Wayne in his roles I did not understand his benign humor in how he treated his image on the silver screen. In fact he seems to poke fun at the very macho role he was acting. I should laugh at myself more - just like John Wayne.

I want to also look at what is really going on in the first film version of The Wizard of Oz, as it traces back to the book by Frank L. Baum.

Dorothy, the Cowardly Lion, the Woodsman (Tin man) and the Scarecrow all believe that the powerful Oz will bring positive change to their lives. Their journey parallels so many of us in America who believe on some level that a higher power can lead us to a type of joyous nirvana.

Look what happens: The impetuous, high strung, pet doggie Toto exposes the booming Wizard of Oz as truly being a chubby, comb-overed, short little meek blow hart who exaggerates with technical tools to control the inhabitants of Oz. The little man is exposed and embarrassed.

What more can be said of the American way? Everyone seems to have a puffed up edifice imposing their will on others. Now being exposed – the little man is to truly act. He must give to the people who ask him for help. This is especially true in the light of his non-admitted powerlessness.

He then gives. He does what he can – as is the American way – (just as in Oz). The little man knows that hope leads to destinations where dreams can come true, but to have dreams come true one must first believe in the hope.

So, what does he do? He fortifies their beliefs and sends each character off fully convinced that their beliefs will lead to the means to find their specifically desired destinations. Hope comes strong.

The Wizard gives a medal of a heart to the Woodsman which causes this Tin Man to have faith and care for others. In America the medical technology to aid patients from cancer to stroke, from a prosthetic limb to a cardiac advance helps so many. We are kept living good and solid lives – especially inspired as those with our military's Purple Heart - awarded for blood and heart valor.

The Scarecrow – the one who is assumed to not have a brain – receives a diploma from the Wizard. The Scarecrow now believes in his abilities and goes on to learn more as he spouts concepts, formulas, and wisdom. There is a special thanks to all who use linguistics and social work as well as self-help, and 12 step programs which keep individuals alive longer than previously assumed. This knowledge adds to life.

The Cowardly Lion needs to believe in himself by standing up and by not being afraid to take action. Heroes are made by those who keep cool heads in dangerous situations. Recognition goes to those who have persistence. To not recognize outstanding work – even when it is labor intensive – means that we do not respect ourselves and what makes up our society. We strive for the good and are led by the best as we stand up for only the best.

Do not settle for less when it comes to your work. Realize with work we turn to our hopes and move towards our dreams. Respect the dreams of others and work with others when you can. The Wizard helped Dorothy and Toto by providing a hot air balloon as they attempt to get back home to Kansas. We want to help all victims. We want to be part of a society that cares to pass on our greatness to each of us in beauty.

Drink a glass of milk. Tap your heels three times. Take a nap and hold hands. Let the magic work for you

2013 Postscript

I have left space in this book for three short ending sections:

I hope that aspiring political cartoonists will submit to me humorous cartoons targeting the humor surrounding mental health in the workplace. For example ideas could range from preconceived notions about patient workers ranging to in enforceable laws which govern employment. I wish to choose the most positively humorous and publish them. An important side-effect would be to help reduce exaggerated stigma, as well as bolster confidence for the mentally and emotionally challenged. I wish to make fun of the situation of the diseases and not the people involved.

I listed four psychiatrists (and there were more) who helped me become well in my introduction to psychotherapy. Each doctor helped in their own way find insights and good health while showing me caring and respect, as I met with them. They helped me solve my own problems. Their input and patience with knowledge of medicine helped me recover. They were able to meet me at each maturity level as I became older. Their therapies were cogent to where I was at any given point of time. I thank each one so much: K. Kovacic M.D., V. Gurijala M.D., S. Poritsky M.D. and K. Weller M.D. The teams that went with them were excellent as well. All those understanding people have kept me alive. I offer praise to the many good medical professionals. Thank You for my life.

In the late 1990's I was asked to visit some local public high schools with Ms. Kim Tresscott – a representative from the National Alliance for the Mentally Ill in Delaware. We attempted to discuss the role of people with mental diagnoses to students in psychology classes. I wanted to be at my best since I was representing the norm of a mental patient. I had wished to include some reaction essays by students but did not receive clearance in time for the first printing.

The experience shows that education about Mental Health is desperately needed. Misconceptions can start at any age. We need to talk more about mental health in our country at all levels.

Finally I want to write about just where Leslie Jeanne and I are now. We live in the same condominium apartment in North Wilmington where we have lived for twenty-five years. This summer we will celebrate twenty five years of marriage and plan to take a trip to Niagara Falls. (Our many Teddy Bears will guard our condo while we are gone).

On a daily basis we share our love and spend time discussing everything from the mundane to the extravagant. This does not mean that we don't have our own personal routines to handle for we have our own responsibilities. Our living relatives are good to us; while Misty – our kitty remains feisty as ever.

We attend our local Catholic Church – Church of the Holy Child and sometimes go to services at the local Christian Science church. A prayer life is very important to us.

Psychologically we are not anywhere near as desperate as we were years ago. Routines have helped in our lives – but truthfully we are so very thankful that you are here too.

Thank You and my God Bless You

Love live the Teddy Bears.

Teddy Bear Finale

I have been asked what is to be done with the teddy bears in this book

Just as in ancient Greek plays where a "chorus" is used to speak directly to the audience, so too have I used teddy bears to speak to my readers.

Shakespeare used witches in <u>Macbeth</u> and gravediggers in <u>Hamlet</u> to provide transitions and give messages to playgoers. Included in the comedy The <u>Taming of the Shrew,</u> the character Biondello consistently makes asides to the audience in hopes that people will be given understanding.

Teddy bears are given in love and attract caring. They are the opposite of violent bombs. They are to humans what angels can be considered to God. Good vulnerable people use teddy bears for comforting.

Teddy bears will always be with us. They show that innocence is present. What do you want to do with sacred innocence?

I feel that only if we teach calmly through expression can we remain sacred. Long live the teddy bears.

"Teribear" "TED E. BEAR"
ALIAS
"MR. TEDDIEST"

Leslie J. Franz

" Critical Attitudes lengthen the miles,
while TOLERANCE AND patience
              bring warm smiles."

Robert R. Franz

In Thanks:

I am forever grateful to my lovely wife Leslie. This book is about our love.

Secondly I give so much thanks to people who through their constant goodness have enabled and motivated me to work my hardest and move me to try and be my best. Audwin Odom, Nan Bernardo, Jennifer Battistone and Omar Rashada have truly taught me that when the student becomes ready -- the teachers will appear. These Counselors, and others like them, through the years prove that people can be spurred forward by simple methods of example and talk therapy. My current psychiatrist knows and helps me with my desires to keep reducing medicine. Her name is Heather Kennedy M.D. and she is very good at her business.

I also give my utmost thanks to Victoria Boyer for preparing this manuscript and Daniel Lacey for the initial marketing. Eric Gryzbowski, Tom McDonough and Carol Buccio have given good suggestions as well. Francis Battaglia brought me a beautiful chair to keep me seated at the computer. I thank all who have given heartfelt support. Sally Todorow, Dr. Michael Wahl, and Thomas Lagana have read this manuscript with interest. Help also came from Larry McKay who added support and expertise in helping me integrate documents and images. Lauren DeGrosky aided with her knowledge of computer science, and finally Alison Boettcher from Union Press has done fine work with the cover. Not one person is in any way unimportant.

All my grateful thanks also go to Jeffrey Geller M.D., M.P.H. and his team of editors for their excellent work. Thank you to all these people.

I am in love with you all, and you who may read this work. Most importantly I thank all of my family, especially my original family – Leslie, Dad, Mother and Annette – for giving me the strength and compassion to travel through life.

Thank you,

Robert N. Franz III

Made in the USA
Middletown, DE
28 July 2015